SIMENON'S PARIS

TEXT BY
GEORGES SIMENON
DRAWINGS BY
FREDERICK FRANCK

SIMENON'S PARIS

THE DIAL PRESS · NEW YORK · 1970

For Harry Torczyner

Bookdesign: Joost Hesseling
Printed in Holland
by N.V. Grafische Industrie Haarlem.

Georges Simenon
XI 68

Frederik Franck
Epalinges; Vaud.

DURING THE WAR, WANDERING THROUGH NEW YORK OR
Pittsburgh, San Francisco or Melbourne, suddenly the darkness of an
alley, a sky of particular luminosity, a moon reflected in black water,
would whip my latent nostalgia for an unreachable Europe into a
pain as acute, as excruciating, as an attack of lumbago.

Europe to me was a Dutch meadow swept by sun under stormy
clouds. It was a tarred barge mirrored in a Belgian canal. And, of
course, it was the Rue Jacob, the Ile Saint-Louis, the cheese stalls of
the Rue Saint Antoine, the bar in the Rue Lepic. Paris. My craving
for Europe was like the longing for a loved woman, a craving that is
not alleviated but sharpened by rereading a last love letter over and
over again. Yet that love letter is one's dearest possession, at once
fetish, charm, security, hope and sustenance.

The love letters from a Europe perhaps lost forever which I read and
reread during those years were the novels of Georges Simenon.
Critics may divide his immense output into detective stories and
psychological novels. To me every one of his books was, and still is, a
love letter to life. It is the characteristically European variant of life,
above all the Paris variant, which he has perceived with awe-inspiring
awareness and has evoked with unmatched poignancy.

Much has been said about the atmospheric, impressionistic quality in
Simenon's writing. Of course it is there, and in abundance. But it is
not there for its own sake; it is made up of thousands of perceptions,
perceptions of the textures on old buildings suffused with sunlight, or
rain and fog, but these are never dissociated from the perceptions of the
light and fog in human eyes and in the human voices that speak the
sparse dialogues.

For me Simenon is first of all the man who perceives with prodigious
sensitivity both the human animal and its lair. The artist in him
transcends the writer, however formidable a writer he may be. It is
the artist who allows his authentic vision to determine the form and
content of his writing and who from this idiosyncratic vision of what
is most particular, most private in each thing, in each being, creates
what is universally and humanly valid.

I have done hundreds of drawings of Paris since the war ended. I had
never been aware of an affinity between my vision and that of
Georges Simenon until one day when I stood drawing on the Place
Maubert, where this book was destined to be born. For a man looked
over my shoulder and said: *"Mais c'est du pur Simenon ce que vous
faites!"* I reacted with what has become my reflex of defense when

onlookers disturb me. I protectively pressed the drawing pad against my chest and gave the art lover a withering look which, I have learned, makes cardinals and even policemen feel guilty of morbid and indecent curiosity. Unfortunately I have not the faintest idea what he looked like, this man who inspired my book. Later that night, in my bed in the little Hotel de Touraine that has become my Paris home, his words came back to me: "That is pure Simenon, what you are drawing there! .." Before I fell asleep this book had taken shape in my mind. After all, many of the drawings were already in my portfolio. What remained to be done was the practical business of assembling, organizing, coordinating the contents of my portfolio with what was in my head.

The drawings in this book are definitely not illustrations. One might as well say that Simenon's texts are illustrations of my drawings. Of course, I had to reread some fifty of Simenon's novels, written with Paris as their setting. As I read them, quite naturally as by a kind of free association, I found the passages that fit my drawings and where my drawings fit his descriptions. Sometimes, in fact, the fragments I had chosen from those countless pages in which he evokes the streets, courtyards, bars and human fauna of Paris, corresponded in the smallest detail to some of my drawings. At other times they did not, but then drawing and text seemed to sing a sort of duet in counterpoint. Now and again, of course, his text would give me the notion to go do something near the Place Clichy, the Rue Lepic, for instance. And then I would take my sketchbook and the Métro, to draw on the spot what I had already seen in my mind.

The only drawings done specifically for this book are the ones of the courtyards and cellblocks of that sinister prison, La Santé, a hundred-year-old horror of dilapidation and misery. I had the feeling that Simenon's Paris without the Santé would be as incomplete as America without J. Edgar Hoover or England without Scotland Yard. But even these drawings are not illustrations of particular passages so much as evocations of an atmosphere.

I soon found out that nobody had ever been allowed to take even a single photograph in the Santé. To request permission to draw inside this grim establishment was not only hopeless, I was told, but ludicrous. Yet by sheer persistence, and aided by one of those chains of misunderstanding and subterfuge which undermine the efficiency of bureaucracies, I succeeded in getting in—and getting out again. At first I drew in despair with trembling hands. The stern warden stood at my elbow, following every stroke of my pen, in the beginning with grim suspicion, later with muttered expressions of grudging respect: *"Mon Dieu, ça c'est re-mar-quable!"* which I found most gratifying. to the ego.

My drawings in this book are a bouquet to Georges Simenon, in homage to the enchanter who conjured up those European scenes and made them live when I most needed them. Without Simenon I would be a far poorer man.

In selecting the passages I did not discriminate for or against the novels which have Inspector Maigret as their hero. Maigret is that pipe-smoking paradigm of a cop who "without any illusions about men, nevertheless continues to have faith in man" *(Maigret et les Vieillards)* and who, through the years, has always again returned from his retirement to his cozy apartment on the Boulevard Richard Lenoir to solve the most puzzling crimes and save the Republic from moronic District Attorneys.

I savored the fragments I selected, turned them over and over in my mind with delight. Soon I knew them more or less by heart. It seemed artificial to use existing English translations. With Georges Simenon's permission I decided to translate them myself.

It would be silly to pretend that all of Simenon's novels (some 200 under his own name plus 200 more under pseudonyms) are on the same level of excellence. An awesome number, however, are undisputed masterpieces: *Les Volets Verts, L'Ours en Peluche, Les Anneaux de Bicêtre, Le Chat, Le Petit Saint, Le Président,* to name but a few. Yet is there a single Simenon, be it the most modest Maigret story, where the unavoidable routine does not conceal a jewel? It may be the evocation of a staircase in a brothel, of a dusk in the Ile Saint-Louis, or the graphic summary of a human face, which makes one realize one is in the presence of a great artist who always succeeds in activating one's own awareness of the multiplicity, the joy, the despair, the grace of being human.

I catch myself thinking, "any Simenon". Indeed, one does not say, "Tonight I'd rather stay home and read a Balzac, a Tolstoi, a Borges." One does say, however: "Tonight I'd rather stay home and read a Simenon." "A Simenon" has become a species, a brand name, a concept. One speaks of "a Simenon" as one speaks of "a Picasso". There are a sufficient number of "Simenons" to fill a lifetime. There is always one still to be discovered and the human span of life, by the grace of God, is just long enough for one to forget a book like *Une Vie Comme Neuve* in order to have the pleasure of rediscovering it.

Neither Simenon nor I are native Parisians, but we share an abiding love for Paris, knowing her all too well to idealize her in the least. Also, I believe that we both prefer to think of her the way she was before the highrisers encircled her and replaced the stark and intimately human *banlieux* with their sad little vegetable gardens, long before she had to prove her excruciating contemporaneity with New York by sprouting hideous skyscrapers on Montparnasse. Perhaps we know Paris better than most Parisians, for love makes for seeing . . .

We also share a native soil. We were born as neighbors in that "land without frontiers" where Holland, Belgium and Germany meet. Simenon was born in the ancient city of Liège in Belgium. I was begotten some years later in Maastricht, some fifteen miles to the North, across the Dutch border. Both of us, as children, watched the Meuse River flow by, swollen in winter until it flooded the quays of both Liège and Maastricht. Both cities share nearly two thousand years of kinship, both saw the Roman legions and Charlemagne ford their river, and both are proud of their Burgundian heritage.

Simenon and I both left the cities of our birth and wandered all over the world, lived in Africa, the Pacific and America, yet we never succeeded in severing our roots, so well embedded were they in this arch-European soil.

In a way Liège is my home town too. I was so nearby that as a schoolboy I often bicycled there, bought chips in that very Rue Léopold where Simenon was born, and pedalled back home to Maastricht.

I am sitting in his study, in the enormous white villa which Simenon has built in a tiny village just above Lausanne in Switzerland. Fifty polished pipes are arranged neatly in a rack on the wall, another ten are carefully laid out on his desk. The room is rather severe and forbidding in its orderliness.

Dusk tints the snowy terrace a bluish violet. In the valley lights are winking on. The Alps in the distance change from cobalt to Prussian blue.

The person sitting in the armchair opposite me, drinking a glass of tea, is a quiet man of sixty-five. It is very hard indeed to believe that this man, who looks like a diplomat or a corporation lawyer, this formal man with his almost stylized courtesy, is the same person who has created that seething mass of all too human incarnations and to whom nothing human can possibly be alien. He does not look a bit like the man of whom a Mauriac could say: "I fear that I shall never have the courage to descend into those abysses of the nightmare which Simenon describes with such nearly unbearable artistry." Neither could I imagine him to be "Balzac without the length", as Marcel Aymé describes him. This punctilious man in his austere white house has hidden his inner self almost completely. The house betrays little of his real character beyond, perhaps, a mania for orderliness, and solid good taste. Here he hides behind his carefully constructed image, the image he has projected in numberless well-managed interviews, the legend of his working methods, of the dozens of sharpened pencils at the ready, the few weeks of self-imposed isolation from which he emerges with a novel ready for the printer.

Those gray eyes behind the horn-rimmed glasses, I suddenly realize in a kind of panic, must be registering my smallest movement, that sharp nose has detected the brand of my tobacco, those ears have registered every inflection in my voice, those senses must be continuously perfecting their capacity for perception, awareness, evaluation, formulation. Behind that standardized, nearly anonymous façade lives the extraordinarily rich humanity he has poured into his hundreds of books.

"He is no doctor," writes Jean Renoir. "He doesn't prescribe pills. He doesn't play the philosopher and doesn't climb onto the ornamental balcony to get a better view of the ants below wiggling in that kerosene-soaked antheap. He is not a man of letters, he is one of those kerosene-soaked ants, a conscious one who succeeds in telling his story."

There is one book no Simenon addict can afford to miss, for it solves a bit of the riddle of that "conscious kerosene-soaked ant", who became the most prodigious writer of the century. It is *Je me souviens*. He wrote it for his son Marc, when the doctors had predicted that he would die young from a neart disease, as had Simenon's father, Désiré. *Je me souviens* is the pitiless and compassionate portrait of the milieu of his childhood in Liège; it is at the same time a magnificent evocation of a family, a city and an epoch. It offers an insight into the child predestined to become the mercilessly tortured observer as he became self-aware in the half sleep of that archetypal *petit bourgeois* milieu, provincial and early twentieth century.

Je me souviens is a poem, not a sociological study. One cannot help agreeing with Jean Cassou who wrote as early as 1932: "There is more poetry in the jazz opera of Kurt Weill or the miraculous novels of Georges Simenon than in most books which pretend to contain poetry because they are printed in irregular lines."

And André Gide once wrote to him: "You enjoy a false reputation, as did after all Baudelaire and Chopin. Nothing is more difficult than to make the public reconsider a first hurried impression. You are still the victim of your first successes and the readers' laziness would like to see there the end of your conquest. My whole lecture wishes to prove that you are a much more important writer than one likes to believe."

To the artist Simenon and to the Paris of the heart he evokes, this book is dedicated.

But now let Simenon speak for himself.

Frederick Franck

We lived in two rooms where everything had to take place, the kitchen and the bedroom. Two rooms easy to heat with human warmth. The ticking of a banal alarm-clock was enough to make the small space come alive. The least bit of wind in the chimney made the stove roar. There were all the familiar squeaks you hear only in that type of old apartment. We had a wardrobe for instance, painted imitation oak, which squeaked all through my childhood, for no explicable reason, at the most unlikely moments.

The sign outside of Grandfather Simenon's shop was an enormous red top hat with gold piping. I was not allowed ever to walk in through the shop itself. Forbidden. I had to enter through the whitewashed passage next to it, where there was always a stale odor from the lavatory. In the kitchen through the glassed wall I saw the beef stew simmering on the stove. Grandma Simenon, I seem to remember, was the only woman who really had the secret of making beef stew.

My grandmother Simenon had the same stone-colored complexion as my grandfather, she was also as cold as stone. I can't remember her ever kissing me. I can't remember either seeing her in a dressing gown or all dressed up. She always wore gray, slate gray. Her hair was gray. Her hands were gray. She wore a single gem, a gold medallion that

Je me souviens

contained a photo of one of her children who had died young. She was of the purest Walloon stock, daughter and granddaughter of miners. My grandfather too had been a miner in his day and still had those telltale little blue spots under his skin.

Nobody said a word. We were sitting together in the kitchen, but no one felt the need to talk. On the wall, a large clock in a brass frame with a big pendulum that, coming and going carried a spot of sunlight along; its hands moved in little jerks, each one accompanied by a metallic click.

My father Désiré is the most intelligent one of the family, and the best educated. He has received a classical education all the way up to the last year of Secondary School. He has to write all the really important official letters for his brothers and sisters and even for the neighbors. He is "in insurances," an expert who counsels the customers.

At the office, in the Rue des Guillemins, too, he is crucially important. No one would challenge his superiority, proven by the fact that he takes home the office keys. The proprietor, Monsieur Mayeur, lives in the Rue des Guillemins, in a large, joyless house built of freestone. The offices form a kind of annex to the house and have their entrance, a heavy door with ornamented nailheads, on the Rue Sohet. A garden separates both buildings. Monsieur Mayeur is in ill health, has always been in ill health and sad, like his mother with whom he lives and who—strange coincidence—is the terror of the salesgirls of the "Innovation", the department store where she spends her afternoons. Monsieur Mayeur bought an insurance agency as an investment, but at least as much in order not to appear to be doing nothing. Désiré already was part of the business when it changed hands.

At two minutes to nine, the moment Désiré opens the door, he undoubtedly has a feeling of dignity, a special satisfaction, that makes him into a different human being, a second Désiré Simenon as real as the other one and as important, for his office work takes up nine hours a day. It is not just a job, any kind of job, a drudgery, a mere way of making a living. Désiré started in that office the day he left school, when he was seventeen. He was to die in it at forty-five alone behind his wicket. The part of the office open to the public was separated by a partition as in a postoffice and he felt a definite satisfaction in belonging inside the partition. The barred windows of opaque, green glass made the street invisible and created an atmosphere all its own. Before even taking off his hat and coat, Désiré always wound the clock. He hated clocks that had stopped. He did everything with the same precision and with the same quiet joy. Washing his hands at the little fountain behind the door was a luxury, a caress. With a kind of delight he took off the cover of the large typewriter, arranged erasers, pencils, carbon paper on the desks.

Your poor grandfather, dear Marc, was a happy man. Happy in his family which was as he envisaged it. Happy in the streets where he

envied no one, happy in the office where he knew himself to be
number one. I really think that every day he lived through an hour
and a half of perfect bliss. It started at noon when Verdier, Lardant
and Lodemans took off like released pigeons. My father stayed alone,
for the office remained open without interruption from 9:00 a.m. to
6:00 p.m. He himself had insisted on staying during lunch time. He
might have ordered someone else to replace him. Customers were
rare at lunchtime and so he had the office to himself. He always
brought coffee in a little bag and put his kettle on the stove. Then in
a corner, his newspaper spread in front of him, he slowly nibbled at
his sandwich and sipped his coffee. By way of dessert he then took
up some delicate or difficult problem that demanded complete quiet.
I even know—because often without telling mother I went to see
him to ask for some spending money—that he took off his jacket
and so, in his shirt sleeves, he felt completely at home.

We are having clear soup, roast beef, applesauce and chips. That is
what we always get on Sundays. The house seems emptier than on
weekdays. The streets too. Our boarders have gone off to the country. Doors and windows stay open. You walk from sunny spots into
shadow spots, from puffs of warm air into puffs of cool air. You
know that soon, in a few minutes, the quarrel is bound to start. Isn't
it funny, you feel it coming! One knows it is useless, and horrible
and absurd and still, there is nothing in one's power that can prevent
it. The incident that sets it off, idiotic as it may seem, simply will
happen. Will Christian, all dressed up in his Sunday best, wet his new
shorts? Will I get my best suit dirty? Or will Désiré mumble:
"Look here, Henriette, it is already two o'clock. Are we ever going to
leave?"

We sit down. My father leans back on his chair, his legs are so long.
Across the street the windows at the attorney's are even more
thoroughly covered with lace curtains than at auntie's. My parents
have brought a cake. We eat it before Vespers. Coming back from
church, the pungent odor of cheese is still hanging in the room.
"Why don't you stay for dinner? "
"We don't want to give you any trouble, Françoise."
My mother is pathologically afraid of giving people trouble. She always sits on the edge of her chair.
"But really, Henriette . . ."
"All right then, then let us get the cold meats at Tonglet's . . ."
It is close by, on the corner of a little street, which decent people
avoid. Ten years, twenty years later, wherever she is living, mother
will still assert that only Tonglet had good cold meats, especially
their *foie piqué*. We have brought along an oval earthenware dish. In
another shop we buy fifty centimes worth of chips and cover them
with a napkin.

They love one another and so they are happily married. But while
Désiré is conscious of this happiness and enjoys it in little puffs,

15

like the puffs of his pipe in the evening, my mother cannot rejoice in *Je me souviens*
happiness. She suffers, because she is used to it, she suffers out of
habit, out of vocation, she always lives in fear of falling short. She
suffers in advance from the idea that she may have let the peas burn
or else that they won't be seasoned well enough, or she worries about
having forgotten some dust in a corner. She suffers when she takes
me to the chemist to have me weighed and she is anxious how she
will break it to Désiré that perhaps I might have lost a few ounces
or maybe failed to gain weight. She dresses me up and since there is
nothing special to do and father is at the office, we go across the
Pont des Arches, the bridge over the Meuse and to the "Innovation",
the department store where she used to work before her
marriage. Yet, there too she had suffered. She was far from sturdy
and after a few hours behind the counter, she was always plagued by
backaches. Even now, in the evening she complains of an aching back
from carrying me, from doing the laundry or from lugging coal and
water upstairs. It is the illness of poor women, of poor mothers.

"Georges, if you are naughty they'll put me into the hospital
again! "
You can't imagine, my poor mother, what horrible nightmares your
little blackmail gave me, how at night, trying to fall asleep, I had to
fight desperately the horrible visions that overwhelmed me.
It was even worse when at other times you threatened: "If you tease
your little brother once more, I'm going to have an operation."

Next to us is the house of the Lamberts, who are "people of independent means." They really have "independent means" and what I mean
is that they were born that way, that it is their natural condition. It
is not that they are old and retired, that they are people resting after
a lifetime of work. They have never done any work. They own titles,
stocks and bonds. They are owners of a number of sordid tenements
in backstreets and everyone knows that is the best investment,
because the poor in the end always pay their rent. The Lamberts
spend their lives in the loggia. Old Mr. Lambert sits there sunning
himself, except when he walks his dog. Old Mrs. Lambert embroiders
or crochets. Miss Lambert, who is going on forty and looks so
distinguished, does what her mother does. The dog, an enormous
magnificent sheep dog, lies on the sidewalk all day long.
Well, hardly is my mother in the street, when she looks up at the
loggia. She smiles her most discreet smile. Then she bends over
towards the dog and pets him. She looks up once more and her smile
becomes a precisely calculated greeting and is allowed to gain in
meaning as Mrs. Lambert nods in turn and Miss Lambert leans
forward for a moment, and sometimes even waves at me.
My father would say, in fact he does say: "They shouldn't leave a big
dog like that running around unmuzzled." My father, after all, is a
Simenon and those little signals between loggia and sidewalk have no
meaning whatsoever to him. But this is what they mean: "Look,
there is that young mother who lives next door on the third floor.

She is taking her toddlers for a walk. Quite a little woman to bring
up two kids on a third floor and to keep them looking that neat!
Isn't she frail! She must be exhausted! But you have to admit that
she has pride and courage! Shouldn't we really show her sympathy
and smile at her children? Isn't the older one thin? At last there is
still somebody who is well-behaved and respectable!"
My mother Henriette then puts these shades of meaning into her
mute reply: "You can see, I hope, that I feel most appreciative of
your solicitude! You at any rate understand me! I do all I can and I
have to do it with only the strict necessities! You are people of
independent means, the richest people in the street, you have a
loggia! I'm really grateful for your showing me your approval! And
to prove that I am not thankless, that I am well brought up, I stroke
your huge dog who, to be truthful, frightens me to death and who
some day could well pounce on my poor children. Thank you!
Thank you very much! Believe me, I am most appreciative . . ."
Forgive me, poor Mother, but this is the truth and I just hope that
your grandson will be liberated of those burdens that weighed on
your shoulders all your life. To prove that it is a true picture:
You haven't walked ten yards farther down the street, when your
glance goes across the street to the other house that has a loggia. It is
not the judge, however, who is acknowledging your mute greeting,
nor his wife, for he is a bachelor. It is his housekeeper, which
amounts to practically the same, for she is not the kind of woman
who goes shopping without a hat. She is a very dignified lady, who
also spends her afternoons sitting in the loggia and who smiles at me.
"What a lovely baby!" she says one day, bending over Christian's
pram. From that moment on, there is no more room for doubt:
Christian really is a lovely baby!
A woman like that Mrs. Loris, however, may be standing at her door,
looking for you, she may overflow with affection and have her apron
pockets full of sweets for me, but her you don't repay with anything
but a reserved little smile that means: "Thank you. I thank you out
of politeness. It is impossible not to, but please understand: we do
not belong to the same world. The Lamberts wouldn't dream of
taking the trouble to greet you from their loggia, neither would the
judge's housekeeper. Everybody in the neighborhood is aware, that
you lived with Loris long before he married you. And everybody
knows that you come from nothing, that you were some kind of
domestic and that you have the worst accent around here. So I do
say 'thank you.' But I feel highly uncomfortable having the other
people see you talking to me. I'd much rather pass by without being
accosted . . ."

The following period lasted until the Second World War. It was a lighter, sunnier time. Dresses had become shorter and women freer. He had discovered Paris slowly, had made his way in it. He had never been bored watching the spectacle of the great boulevards. It seemed to him as if at that time we were less worried about life, about our personal problems than now. Or was that perhaps just because we all were so much younger? Didn't people feel they were part of a game, weren't they less committed to what they did or didn't do?

In 1940 we were dispersed in all directions. Some fled to the non-occupied zone, to England or America. When at long last the Allied troops paraded on the Champs-Elysées, we could make up the balance sheet. There were many empty spots. Some had died in concentration camps. Some had become heroes and others, considered to have been collaborators, didn't dare to show themselves anymore. One had been shot by the Committee of Liberation. The great Boulevards no longer were the heart of Paris. It had become the turn of the Champs-Elysées, where cars were invading the sidewalks. For the smallest trifles people were taking planes to New York or Tokyo Why do we have the uncomfortable feeling that the sky is darkening again? Is it the threat of atomic war? Is it the ever more accelerated rhythm of our lives, where girls wear the same blue jeans as boys and it is said that both now look on love as a branch of acrobatics?

Les anneaux de Bicêtre

That poor Boulevard Richard-Lenoir! What on earth has given it that bad reputation? All right, so it does end at the Bastille. Okay, so it is surrounded by miserable slummy little streets. The whole section is full of workshops and warehouses. But the Boulevard itself is wide, it even has grass in the middle, even though it grows on top of the métro with its smelly entrances that are spewing chlorinated air! Every two minutes, as a train rumbles by, the houses are seized by a strange shudder. But one gets used to it. Friends and colleagues, during the last thirty years or so, had spoken highly of cheerful apartments in friendlier surroundings. He went to see them and grumbled: "Very nice, very nice . . ."

"And look at that view, Maigret! "

"Yes, yes . . . "

"And don't you like those large, sunny rooms?"

"Well, yes . . . it really is lovely . . . I wouldn't mind living here at all . . . but . . ." and he took his time before sighing, shaking his head: "but it would mean moving! "

Too bad for those who despise the Boulevard Richard-Lenoir.

Maigret et son mort

Un échec de Maigret

Nobody had ever known a March that had been as cold, wet and dismal. At eleven in the morning, the offices were still bathed in a melancholy half-light, reminding one of an execution at dawn. At noon the lights were still on and at three o'clock dusk had fallen again. There was no sense in saying that it was raining, one lived in a cloud. Water was everywhere, the floors had puddles. People were incapable of saying three consecutive words without blowing their noses. All the newspapers printed photographs of suburbanites going home in rowboats through streets that had become rivers.

"Where did you meet monsieur Louis? "
"On a bench on the Boulevard Bonne-
Nouvelle."
"How did you get to know each other? "
"The way one gets to know people on
benches; I said to him 'Spring is coming' and
he said that the air was warmer than last
week."
"And who got the idea? "
"Him of course. Actually it was that bench
that gave him the idea."
"What do you mean?"
"He was always sitting on that same bench,
day after day, and so after a while he began
to notice things around him. I don't know if
you know where that rainwear store is on
the boulevard. Well, the bench where Louis
used to sit is right across from it. So that,
without even trying, he got to know the
comings and goings in that store and he
knew the habits of every salesman. That gave
him the idea. If you have nothing to do all
day long, you think and think and you make
plans, even plans that you know will never
come true. So one day, just to pass the time
away, he talked to me about his plans. That
store is always full of people. It is stuffed
with raincoats in all styles for men, women
and children. On the second floor they have
even more. Now on the left of the building,
there runs one of those alleys you find
everywhere in that neighborhood. It ends in
a kind of courtyard.

"Louis had been watching that store for
weeks on end. Before they closed for lunch,
they never took the trouble to check in all
the corners, behind those thousands of
raincoats, whether someone was staying
behind. They just never got the idea that a
customer could have himself locked in. See
what I mean . . . So Louis says to me: 'Can
you understand why nobody has ever taken
the dough? There is nothing to it.' "

Maigret et l'homme du banc

26

Boulevard Rochechouart

Sure, he used to have a drink in every bar. He drank away a good deal of the little bit of money he got together with so much trouble, by so many little ruses and humiliations. But he began to feel wonderful, like a dog in his basket when the fog became just right, just thick enough. There was a kind of bliss in looking at the world with a woeful envy, in bashing one's head against those proud buildings that looked to him as if they had been built specifically for him to bash his head against.

He was small and weak and on him destiny pounced with fury, pursuing him day after day with huge waves of ferocious laughter at each well-placed blow. As soon as he seemed to get to his feet again, as soon as he caught a ray of hope, the monster quickly as lightning invented a new misfortune to force him back to his knees.

It was easy: the fog was well within reach. Often during those last three years he had looked with longing at every bar, not so much because he wanted a drink, but in order to find once again that precise density of atmosphere for which he always longed. A few glasses on a sticky counter, the air thick with the odour of cheap wine and booze, where he could feel again the most dejected man in all the wide world.

*Les quatre jours
d'un pauvre homme*

It was the first morning that really felt like spring. A woman was selling flowers at the entrance of the métro. The girl on the seat next to him had flowers pinned on her blouse and the fragrance came to him in whiffs.

No one ever smiled at him. He never smiled at anyone. There were people in that train he had travelled with for years, a number of times each week. Some of them nodded vaguely at each other or even exchanged a few words. Not he. Before he got to the Etienne-Marcel station, he had already carefully folded his newspaper. Slipping it into his pocket, he walked to the exit.

Une vie comme neuve

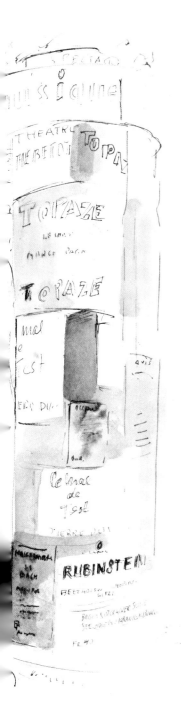

It had been a long time since he had last taken a métro. He emerged from it, depressed by that subterranean clamminess, by that life seen as in slow motion, in a light without brilliance and without shadow, a world mute like the world of fishes, where the only noise was the metallic roar of the trains.

At the bottom of the stone steps, where an enamel sign ordered him to keep left, the glare of daylight hit him and from that angle, he didn't immediately recognize the columns of the Madeleine. He stopped halfway up the steps and discovered another aspect of the universe, as seen from the level of the sidewalk. Thousands of legs were in motion, brightly colored legs of women, with high heels tapping rhythmically as in a dance, dark fluttering men's legs; and, like the roar of surf, the crashing of all those soles on the dirty pavement, the shrieks of brakes of cars and buses. It was as if in the short time since he had gone underground, life's rhythm had been accelerated. As he crossed the boulevard he felt awkward.

Les quatre jours d'un pauvre homme

The more elegant Parisians are, the later they dine and when The
Mouse got as far as Fouquet's on the corner of the Champs-Elysées
and the Avenue Georges V, some two hundred people were having
cocktails on the terrace. Many of them were still carrying the field
glasses they had used that afternoon at the races of Maisons-Laffitte.
The old duffer had some trouble catching his breath, was a bit
baffled by that crowd and thought it wise to case the joint before
pulling the New York *Herald* out of his pocket.

"Excuse me, ladies and gentlemen . . . you couldn't spare a couple of

Monsieur La Souris   francs for a drink to your health? "

That was the best method he could think of, the only one at his
disposal to get a close look at everybody, especially now that there
was no uniform in sight. He hobbled around a bit, threaded his way
between the tables, avoiding the waiters, who in that kind of
establishment are worse than cops. He had trouble smiling, because
he was still out of breath.

"My respects, Your Highness . . . I bet you have too much small
change in your pocket . . . Nothing is worse for one's clothes! "

His whole bag of tricks . . . Never arouse pity, always make people
laugh!

"If I had known you were going to Maisons-Laffitte, sir, I'd have
given you a good tip for the third race. The jockey and me, we are
like twins, see . . . ."

32

"One day in July, during the exams, I was sitting with a boy friend on the terrace of the Harcourt on the Boulevard Saint-Michel. He was a Rumanian student who was going back home for the holidays. July and August were always tough months to get through for me. Sometimes I even tried to hook tourists on the great Boulevards. And once I got myself arrested for soliciting and I still don't know by what miracle I got out of it. I looked so young at the time that the inspector before whom we had to appear took pity on me. You don't mind if I take another little glass, do you?"

And then she asked, sitting down again:

"I am not shocking you, am I?"

"Not a bit."

"Then admit that you always suspected me of it!"

"Right!"

"Now let me tell you how I met Bob, although nobody called him Bob yet. As I said, I was sitting on that terrace with my Rumanian. It was late in the afternoon and it was very crowded; a tall young man with reddish-blond hair and light gray eyes came by. Those gray eyes struck me immediately, and the fact that his clothes went so well with those eyes: he had a suit of the same gray, a tie and even socks to match. He stopped for a moment to shake hands with my friend, just vaguely looked at me and went to the bar. He was not at all the Bob you have known. He looked more like that young nephew of his you saw the other day.

"Who is he?" I asked my friend.

"He interests you?"

"Well, he has extraordinary eyes . . ."

Le grand Bob

33

Jublin must have joined the group around 1928, a bit before Besson d'Argoulet and at any rate it was when wē still used to meet in the Brasserie Graf. He was a tall emaciated boy who, at a costume ball given by a painter in his studio on the Boulevard Rochechouart, played Boneless Valentin, the famous quadrille dancer of the Moulin Rouge, the one painted by Toulouse-Lautrec. Jublin's face, which had a chalky pallor, remained imperturbable even during his most extravagantly witty remarks. He was four or five years older than Maugras, had been part of the early Dada movement and had later become a Surrealist.

He actually lived in cafés, never attached himself to a particular group, nor to a particular section of Paris. He could be found as well in the "Deux-Magots", Boulevard Saint-Germain, as in the bars of the Champs-Elysées or the bistros of Montmartre. He knew everybody, but nobody really had any idea of him.

Les anneaux de Bicêtre

34

Although dusk had not yet fallen, it was as if a
haze floated through the studio. The towers of
Notre-Dame, recently cleaned, stood chalk white
against a nearly black sky. From time to time one
heard the hooting of tugboats. Here and there
lights began to glimmer throughout the cityscape.
Sophie, lying on a couch near the window, had lit
a cigarette. Her grandmother, as if on a visit, was
sitting very straight in one of the satin armchairs.
"Aren't you going to dress? "
"No."
"But you are going to have dinner in town, aren't
La vieille   you? "

They stopped once more at the narrow end of the
Ile Saint-Louis, opposite the drowsy mass of
Notre-Dame. Then they crossed the Pont Marie,
where some barges were anchored, lying side by
side like couples. On the bridge, each one of them
was spreading the yellow light of a ship's lantern.
Nelly didn't ask him whether he felt that light-
headedness again. Consciously she avoided
watching him from the corner of her eye, as she
often found herself doing in the midst of city
crowds. It seemed that he now felt freed from
those disturbing thoughts which made him feel
contemptible. When his wife was not close to him,
those thoughts overpowered him. Then all he had
ever said and done in the past, as well as in the
present, seemed to assume a quite different
La porte meaning.

37

Two or perhaps three times that afternoon Maigret looked up from his papers and gazed at the sky. It was limpid blue, in it floated white clouds fringed with gold. Sunlight was pouring over the roofs. Then he stopped his work, sighed and opened his window. Hardly had he sat down again, inhaling a breath of spring that gave a special fragrance to his pipe, when the papers on his desk started to tremble, to take flight and to land all over his room.

The clouds no longer were white and gold, but had changed to slate blue and sheets of rain fell diagonally, making bubbles on the windowsill. On the Pont Saint-Michel people suddenly started running as they do in old silent films and women were holding their skirts down.

The second time it was not rain that fell, but hailstones big as ping-pong balls bounced back from the stones, and when he jumped up to close the window again the floor was covered with them.

Maigret et la jeune morte

And then, one day, one evening, one found
oneself on a café terrace or on a bench or
walking along a street with a human being
one had no idea existed the day before.
"What are you thinking about? "
"I'm thinking of you, you are a funny boy."
"What do you mean, I'm funny? "
"Do you often walk with a girl without
saying a word? "
"No, this is the first time."
"So why with me? "
"Don't know . . ."
It must be because she is different. And then
she starts telling him about herself. Each in
turn rushes to tell the other about himself.
They discover their differences. Even the
skin is different, and the nose and the eyes
and the ears and especially the mouth, which
one has to savor the taste of as soon as
possible. Then come the breasts and all that
one is in such a hurry to try and feel . . .
even the sighing is different.
"I love you."
"I love you even more."
"How could this have happened? "
"It just had to."
That horribly icy moon even looks poetic.
"What would have happened if chance had
not brought us together? "
"My life would never have been the same."
"Mine either."
"It would have been empty like that of most
people. Very few people ever get to know
real love! "
"How awful that must be."
"They are lucky they don't know."
"You really think so? "
"If they knew it, don't you think they
would shoot themselves? "
"You're terrible."
"I love you."

L'homme au petit chien

It was good to sleep. It was especially good to have those dreams in which he had no age, in which he was not old. It sometimes happened that in his dreams he saw landscapes as he saw them long ago. Landscapes that were alive with vibrant color, from which arose delicious fragrances. Sometimes in these dreams he was running, out of breath, to find the spring whose soft murmurings he had heard.

He never dreamed of Marguerite and very rarely of his first wife. And when that happened, he always dreamed of her as she had been just before their marriage.

Did Marguerite dream too? Of her first husband perhaps? Of her father? Of the time when she used to wear those wide-brimmed straw hats and walk along the Marne under a parasol? What did he care! Let her dream about her first husband, that musician, and of her childhood if she felt like it.

What did it mean to him anyway . . .

Le chat

Ambassador Armand de Saint-Hilaire, on the other hand, didn't try in his letters to make her believe in his own chastity.

Princess Isabelle wrote to him, for instance: *"I do hope those Turkish women are less passionate than their reputation and I hope especially that their husbands are not as savage . . ."* She added: *"Be very careful, darling. Every morning I pray for you . . ."*

When he was *chargé d'affaires* in Cuba and later ambassador in Buenos Aires, she worried about women with Spanish blood: *"Are they really so beautiful? And I, so far away from you, somewhere in the background . . . I tremble to think that one day you are going to fall in love . . ."*

She was also anxious about his health: *"Are your boils still giving you much pain? In that heat it must be . . ."*

She knew his housekeeper, Jaquette. *"I'm going to write to Jaquette to give her the recipe of that almond cake you are so fond of . . .*

Hadn't she promised her husband never to meet Saint-Hilaire again?

"What an indescribable and painful joy I felt when I saw you last night from afar in the Opéra. I just love your graying temples. And now that you have gotten a bit heavier, you look exceptionally distinguished . . . I was so proud of you all evening . . . Only when we got back to the Rue de Varenne and I studied myself in the mirror I became so very frightened . . . You must have been so disappointed looking at me. Women fade so quickly and I am already almost an old woman . . ."

Maigret et les vieillards

44

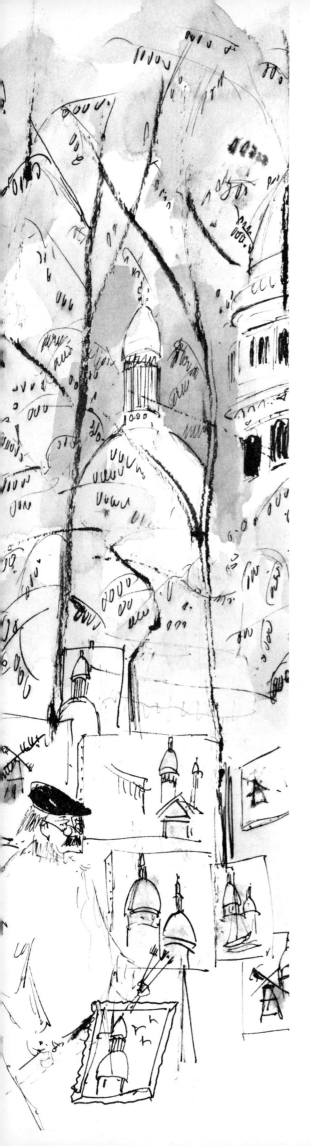

The Place du Tertre looked like a carnival. It was crowded with foreign tourists sitting at the café tables which occupied the entire square. Some poor devils, trying to look like artists, were peddling their portfolios of watercolors from table to table. There were musicians and street singers and on the corner there was even a fire-eater in a skin-tight blue sailor's sweater.

Les volets verts

The Place des Abbesses, much more than the Place du Tertre, which had become nothing but a tourist trap, was typical of the real Montmartre of the people, Inspector Maigret thought, with that little theatre that looked like a toy or a stage set, its bistros, its little shops and its métro entrance. He remembered that he had first discovered it one chilly, but sunny spring morning soon after he had come to Paris. He had felt as if he was walking through a painting by Utrillo. The square was teeming with common folk, people from the neigh-borhood, like villagers going about their business on market day and, like villagers too, they seemed to belong to one large family.

Maigret et le client du samedi

"Come here, Bib."

My dog must have thought for a moment that I wanted to take the cable car. He was already looking at my shopping bag, ready to jump into it, but I decided to walk down the stone steps. People were slowly climbing up, stopping every few steps to catch their breath.

Then suddenly I saw them. I must have passed dozens of couples I had not paid any attention to. This couple was taking the steps very slowly, seen from above they looked even more deformed than in reality. I was struck first by the man's head, a monstrously large head, a hydrocephalic head such as one sees practically only in medical books. His skin was of the same pink as a baby's skin, completely hairless. His protuberant eyes were naked, without eyelashes. Under a nearly normal torso one discovered two tiny legs so weak that they were as if suspended from the trunk. He obviously had the greatest difficulty walking with the help of two crutches and threw out one foot to the left, one to the right, as if each step he conquered was a special feat. Each time he bowed his head to prepare his start, then he looked up to measure the distance he still had to go, as if the white mass of the church of Sacré Coeur, high above, was his life's ultimate aim.

I have not the slightest idea whether he was thirty, forty or older. He was completely outside the normal world of men. It was no doubt a miracle that he had survived at all. His companion, a swarthy little woman with irregular features, wore orthopedic shoes, one of them with iron braced which reached up to her knee.

She was keeping one hand on the man's arm, clearly less to support him than to express tenderness and each time he had conquered another step, she gave him a smile as if to thank him or to congratulate him for a successful effort.

L'homme au petit chien

Le passage de la ligne

The Moulin Rouge in those days, with its illuminated sails turning slowly against the sky of the Place Blanche, and its entrance, more brilliantly lit than all the rest of the boulevard, that always made me think of the open maw of a monster, was an immense ballroom, where every evening ordinary people came to dance. They were not ordinary in the sad, drab sense of the word. Thousands of office girls, salesgirls, little housemaids and young clerks from all over the city could, for a few francs, live in the illusion of luxury and high life for an evening. Nowhere else at that time could one find such an orgy of electric bulbs and projectors. Two orchestras played in turn and exactly at eleven, when the couples were getting tired of waltzing or charlestoning, the floor was suddenly invaded by the frenetic cancan dancers.

At nine o'clock the admission was increased to three francs, I think it was, and later as the house filled up, the admission kept rising until by ten thirty, when the tourists came to watch the cancan or sit at the bar, it had reached its maximum for the night.

The Moulin Rouge era marks a milestone in time, in space, and in depth. Hundreds of ghosts stir in my memory and together form something alive which I find inexpressible in words. One would have to bring to life a whole neighborhood, an entire epoch with its own music, its own fashions, in which not only the silhouette of women was different, but even the expression in their eyes, their smiles, yes, even the shape of their faces.

Around ten thirty a drumroll announced the floor-show. The lights went out, the projectors focused on the dance floor, which was then invaded with a triumphant yell by the cancan dancers in a flourish of flying skirts.

How many were there? Maybe twenty, he thought, each one wearing a different color dress, each one in her turn doing her special number with all the others standing around her, immobile like statues.

The one in red was a lovely brunette with sumptuous breasts and hungry lips; the yellow one a tall adolescent with an unfinished face; the one in purple a real acrobat, who specialized in the most daring jumps. For some twenty minutes there was an orgy of sound, of movement, of multicolored silk, of black stockings against the pallor of white thighs. The green one was Marcelle, anemic and thin, whose number was the least spectacular and who got the least applause.

If he had dared to choose, wouldn't he rather have had the red one with the full lips? He was not sure. He wouldn't have been at ease with her. He would have been afraid. Night after night he had sat there, watching the thin, green chorus girl with a tenderness mixed with pity. Then he had hung around near the stage door after the show. He was disappointed on seeing that the girls in their street clothes were neither more nor less desirable than the salesgirls and the typists who came to dance. Some had a date, not with a wealthy lover in a sumptuous car, but with a youngster who popped out of the shadows, and they walked away arm in arm. Others, like Marcelle, rushed to the métro entrance.

Les anneaux de Bicêtre

Was he in love with her or with the lights of the Moulin Rouge? Or was he perhaps in love with the contrast between the skirts flying as the band burst out in a frenzy and the frightened kid with her schoolgirl's beret, nervously pushing the button at her parents' door?

"You find anything? " Maigret asked, filling his pipe.
"I took a peek. Have a look in the left side of that chest of drawers."
It was full of photographs, all of Arlette. Some were publicity
photos like the ones at the entrance of Picratt's bar, in which she
showed herself in a black silk dress. It was not the one she was found
in, but an extremely clinging evening dress.
"Have you ever seen her number, Lognon, since it was in your
precinct? "

"No, I haven't, but I know what it amounted to. As far as her
'dance' was concerned, as you can see from the photographs, it
meant she wiggled more or less in time with the music and then
crawled out of her dress with nothing underneath. At the end of her
number, of course, she stood there naked as a worm."
Lognon's long bulbous nose almost seemed to tremble and blush.
"They say that's exactly what they do in those burlesques in
America. The moment she had nothing left on, the lights went out." *Maigret au 'Picratt's'*

54

In his fear of being tempted to go and make sure the old woman
with her flowers was still standing in the Rue de Douai, he had gone
instead for that night to a neighborhood at the very opposite end of
town, Les Gobelins. He found it one of the saddest sections of Paris,
with those wide avenues of monotonous flats like army barracks,
neither new nor old, and with cafés crowded by mediocre people,
who were neither rich nor poor.

*L'homme qui
regardait passer les trains*

It was that time late at night when it gets cold and clammy. A light halo stood around the street-lights. Some cars were parked in front of a night-club that was still open on the corner of the Boulevard Raspail. The uniformed doorman at the entrance mistook the two men for possible customers and as he pushed the door, some snatches of music escaped from inside. Nightlife at Montparnasse was not yet over.

Against the wall near a little hotel a couple were having a whispered argument. As the doctor had predicted, the light in the bar was still on. From the outside one saw a few moving shadows. An old flower vendor at the counter was drinking a cup of coffee that smelled strongly of rum.

The doctor was a rather short, broad-shouldered, plump fellow, who probably never lost his self-assurance, his dignity and his amiability. One could sense that he was used to well-to-do, well-mannered patients, spoilt by life; he had adopted their tone of voice and their manners, which he exaggerated a bit.

Maigret et les braves gens

La tête d'un homme

It was teeming with people. A small swinging door at the far end of the café opened and closed uninterruptedly to let olives, chips, sandwiches and warm beverages pass. Four waiters were shouting their orders simultaneously in the midst of the clatter of plates and glasses, while customers were shouting to one another in different languages.

The dominant impression was that here customers, barmen, waiters, and interior formed a homogeneous entity. People elbowed each other unceremoniously and everybody called the barman Bob: the industrialist who got out of his limousine surrounded by jovial friends, the phoney artist, as well as the little pick-up. A German was talking English to a Yankee. A Norwegian was trying in at least three languages to make himself understood by a Spaniard.

In the beginning of our marriage, when we lived on the Place
Denfort-Rochereau with the Lion of Belfort under our window, I
still went to the office by métro. That didn't last very long, about a
year, for afterwards I could afford a taxi. Then it didn't take long
before we bought a second-hand car. Viviane had a driver's license. I
never could pass the test, I have no mechanical aptitude or perhaps I
lack the proper reflexes. I am so tense at the wheel, so concerned
about an inevitable catastrophe, that the inspector who gave me the
test advised me:

"You'd better give up, Monsieur Gobillot. You're not the only one
and nearly always they are people of extraordinary intelligence.
Sure, if you tried again two or three times, you'd get your license
but just as surely one day you'd have an accident. No, it just isn't for
you."

I always remember the respect with which he said those last words. I
was beginning to get a reputation.

A few months, even a few weeks ago, shopping in the neighborhood had still been one of his greatest pleasures. He didn't feel at all ashamed walking around with a shopping bag like a housewife. In the shops where one had to wait one's turn, the few men he noticed were nearly all old, retired people, widowers, lonely bachelors, or husbands of bedridden wives.

He started at the butcher's, for later in the morning there was a chance they would be out of calves' liver. The sun hit the sidewalk full force. It fell on the red painted ironwork and on the red-and-yellow striped canvas, which during the summer was always hanging behind the marble of the shopwindow, hardly leaving sufficient room for the customers to pass through.

La porte

Rue Toitbout

Maigret en meublé

He had not switched on the light right away. After taking off his tie and opening his shirt, he went to the window and leaned out as thousands of other Parisians were surely doing that evening. The air was soft as velvet, you could nearly feel it. Not a movement, not a sound disturbed the peace of the Rue Lhomond, which nearly imperceptibly sloped down towards the lights of the Rue Mouffetard. Somewhere far behind the houses one heard the muffled roar, the vague noise of traffic, of brakes and horns on the Boulevard Saint-Michel, as if penetrating from another world. Between the roofs of houses, between the chimney pots, one could ecstatically escape into an infinity studded with stars.

"You want me to call the doctor? "
He shook his head.
"You don't need anything? "
Same movement. He was not play-acting. He was very far removed from her in a world of incoherence. Around five o'clock she went out again and he went downstairs once more to find something to eat. His legs felt wobbly. His head was turning. He held on to the handrail like a very sick man, afraid of plunging forward. He found a slice of ham in the refrigerator and ate it with his fingers, then he swallowed a piece of cheese. It was Marguerite's food, but she could go out and get herself something else if she wanted to. The next day he knew that it was Sunday, because of the silence. The universe was immobile with only a sound of church bells far away. She had gone to Mass. He didn't feel ill anymore. He was ravenously hungry. He felt above all the need to get rid of his sweaty odor and to have a shave. He was weaker than he had thought, but he took a shower anyway. As he was shaving, his hands trembled.

Le chat

66

She may have had to work for it all her life, but now she had a nest egg. Some of these old domestics don't even trust the bank. They would rather keep their money under their mattress . . . At any rate there would be nothing to it: just turn around, grab her softly by the throat and press as hard as you can . . . It would take at most two and a half to three minutes . . .

'L'outlaw'

That part of the street is at most fifty yards from the Place de la Bastille. The Rue de la Lappe with its dance halls and its dubious poolrooms and taverns ends in it. Every first floor is a bistro, every house a hotel, peopled by drifters, permanently unemployed, emigrants, hoodlums and whores. Still, in the midst of that disquieting sanctuary of the underworld, one finds workshops where all the doors stand wide open and people are hammering, using acetylene torches, while heavy trucks are being loaded and unloaded. What a violent contrast between that active life of regular working men, of employees running around with bills of lading, and those sordid or insolent asocial types in one and the same street.
"Jeunet here? " grunted the inspector, pushing the door of the little hotel office on the dirty mezzanine.
"Not here! "

Le pendu de Saint-Pholien

She was so huge and fat that she filled the whole doorway. She wore a silly little hat with a green pompom. With her two plump hands she was pressing a little girl's pocketbook against her belly. She wore the modest, nearly prim expression of the type of woman one associates with cleaning vegetables or knitting baby things. She was standing there immobile like a piece of sculpture and behind her, halfway down the passage, one could see the glass door with the word "Hotel" surrounded by painted curlicues.
It was in the Rue de la Roquette but at the spot where it ends in the Place de la Bastille. During the day that notorious doorway was hard to find, hidden as it was between the little shops in the building; at night all one saw was that door with the huge woman blocking it, bending forward each time she heard steps approaching. A bit farther, in a doorway just like this one, three of them were standing. They took turns following lonely passersby, often as far as the corner of the Faubourg Saint-Antoine.

'L'outlaw'

There is no caretaker, nor are there other tenants. Every evening from six o'clock on, my dog Bib and I are all by ourselves and on Sundays we are alone all day long. I undo the chain on the door, pull the bolt, and turn the big key that never comes out of the lock. Bib slips out and dashes off as soon as the opening is wide enough to let him through. He rushes to the corner of the house across the street where he lifts his leg. It has been raining. Not really hard, just enough of a shower to blacken the pavement and to pervade the night air with a breath of moisture. I stay on the threshold and light a cigarette. I always have cigarettes and matches in my dressing gown. I don't think, I don't look at anything in particular. Bib and I, the streetlamp on the corner, the two other streetlights a bit further down, we are the components of a stage set. In front of the mirror, under the glare of the naked light bulb, I pull a comb through my hair. It is getting thin and has lately taken on a color I can't quite get used to. It has nothing in common with that silky silver-gray that so often adorns men of my age. My hair has the neutral, dirty shade of an old tarpaulin and through it shines my pallid scalp. I just wonder if other people who are getting old feel that same shock I feel when they look in the mirror in the morning. I find myself so ugly that often I can't help making a face at myself. Maybe I never have been very handsome but still, during a good part of my life, I have been able to look at my image without revulsion. Perhaps I even looked at myself with a bit of secret self-satisfaction. I was tall and muscular with the solid bone structure of all the Allards. Have I really shrunk? Probably. My big body has become flabby, my face puffed up, unhealthy. My eyes remind me of cod eyes in the window of a fish shop.

Don't misunderstand me, I'm not complaining. I am not crying over my fate. It would be a mistake to assume that I regret the past. I am absolutely lucid, so lucid that I can look at myself in the mirror and say aloud:

"You're ugly! "

Having to add sometimes:

"You make me sick! "

L'homme au petit chien

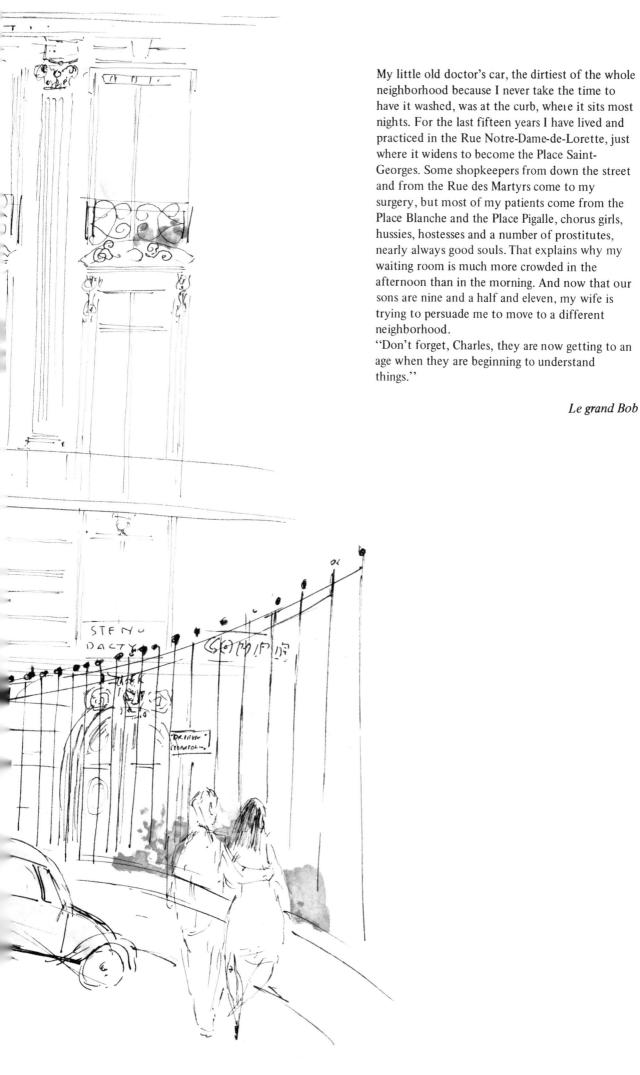

My little old doctor's car, the dirtiest of the whole neighborhood because I never take the time to have it washed, was at the curb, where it sits most nights. For the last fifteen years I have lived and practiced in the Rue Notre-Dame-de-Lorette, just where it widens to become the Place Saint-Georges. Some shopkeepers from down the street and from the Rue des Martyrs come to my surgery, but most of my patients come from the Place Blanche and the Place Pigalle, chorus girls, hussies, hostesses and a number of prostitutes, nearly always good souls. That explains why my waiting room is much more crowded in the afternoon than in the morning. And now that our sons are nine and a half and eleven, my wife is trying to persuade me to move to a different neighborhood.

"Don't forget, Charles, they are now getting to an age when they are beginning to understand things."

Le grand Bob

Maigret et le voleur paresseux

Hundreds, thousands of policemen and *gendarmes* had the picture of the escaped prisoner in their pockets. Detectives went from door to door like encyclopaedia salesmen. "Excuse me, Ma'm, have you seen this man recently? " The hotel brigade took care of hotels and boarding houses. The morals squad questioned the professionals. In the railway stations travelers didn't even suspect that anonymous eyes were scanning them as they went by.

74

It had been all over the papers. Later Robert had spotted the Cousin in Paris, in a café on the Rue Saint-Antoine, somewhere near the Saint-Paul cinema.

And now Chave was looking for that café. The sun was flooding one half of the street and it was fun to watch the salesgirls and shop clerks arranging the colorful stands on the pavement. All possible edibles in immense quantities: piles of meat, of fish, of cheeses, of canned goods, vegetables, pies and other baked goods—all that people eat—in wholesale quantities.

He stopped for a moment in front of a luncheonette not far from the movie theatre, but he didn't see anyone who looked remotely like the Cousin and he was just on the point of giving up, when a slim figure briskly slipped through the crowd and disappeared into *Le suspect* the café.

75

Sure that she was being watched by invisible policemen, the old woman
assumed an air of cheerful unconcern. She wanted to make it clear
to them that she was not the loser in the game, that she did not quit
because they were forcing her, because she had been vanquished, but
that she was leaving of her own free will with all her possessions and
that her rich granddaughter had come to fetch her, because she had
been invited to share the elegant flat on the Ile Saint-Louis.
Surreptitiously she was looking for those men who she felt had been
persecuting her for days and when she joined Sophie, she pointed at
the opaque windows of the bar across the street.
"I bet that's where they are sitting, spying on me."
The next thing she said, innocent as it might appear, betrayed her
real preoccupation at that particular moment.
"What kind of car have you got?"
"I've got three of them. One big American sedan and two Italian
ones."
"Those long, low sporty ones?" Wasn't she secretly very
disappointed that Sophie hadn't come to fetch her in one of those
cars instead of by taxi? All the neighbors would have looked out of
their little shops in awe.   *La vieille*

Rue de Grenelle

When he got to the Rue Thorel, he saw the dull gray of the official building, the flags hanging from their masts, the bicycles of the cops. Two policemen were coming out into the street, tightening their leather belts. One of them gave him a look as if his face reminded him of something or other, then he climbed onto his bike without having found the answer.
He entered the precinct station, where the lights were already on. A thick cloud of pipe and cigarette smoke floated around the light bulbs. A man of undetermined age was trying to make himself understood to the peaked police cap that was sticking out above the high blackened counter.

Le veuf

"Have you or haven't you got a working permit? "
"Looka here, monsieur policeman . . ."
That was about all he could say in French. For the
rest he used incomprehensible words, gesticulated,
fumbled with feverish trembling hands through the
papers full of dirty finger marks that had been
stuffed at random in all his pockets.
". . . he tole me . . ."
"Who told you? "
With a gesture he tried to show that he was talking
about someone either very tall or very important.
"Mister . . ."
"But he didn't tell you, did he, that this is a
working permit, huh? "
Not a single paper was the right one. He had them   *Le veuf*
in white, pink, blue, in French and God knows
what foreign languages.
"How much money have you got on you? "

80

Paris showed the melancholy face it has on ugly
October days: a raw light was falling from a sky
like a dirty ceiling. On the sidewalks remained
traces of the heavy rainfall of the night before.
Passersby too had the grim, unhappy look people
have before they become adapted to wintry
weather.

All night long instructions had been typed at
Headquarters, rushed by messengers to the various
precincts, telegraphed to the *gendarmeries*, to the
customs and the railroad police. Everywhere
policemen were mixing with the crowds, scanning
every face, hoping to find that one man. That was
the way it was from one end of Paris to the other,
in all the suburbs, on all highways where police
were checking people's papers..

La tête d'un homme

81

Right in the middle of Paris at a time when the traffic was still dense! Had they taken him for a ride before shooting him? Probably not. Chances were that they had used a gun with a silencer. A bit later, at any rate, they had pushed the body onto the sidewalk of the Rue Fléchier.

Maigret was doodling stick figures on a sheet of paper like a schoolboy scribbling in the margin of his notebook.

Maigret, Lognon et les gangsters

Outside all was confusion. The hearse was so over-
flowing with flowers and wreathes that two extra
cars had to be found to transport the surplus. All
one could see was a sea of heads, hundreds of
heads and above them somewhere the stiff banner
of the Auvergnats of Paris. Someone—he had no
idea who it could be—limlpy shook hands with
him as he passed by, then he found himself in one
of the limousines with both his brothers. It took
another ten minutes before the funeral procession
could start to move. In the limousine in front of
them he could see the white surplice of the priest
and the blond hair of a choirboy. Slowly they
drove through Les Halles between two hedges of
silent spectators. Then as they reached the Seine,
they started to pick up speed.

La mort d'Auguste

BAINS DOUCHES ST MÉDARD

My first assignment was the railway stations. To be more precise, I was sent to a certain somber and sinister building known as the Gare du Nord. You have the advantage, as in the department stores, that you're not standing outside in the rain. But you're not sheltered from cold or wind, because there is no place in the world which is more drafty than a station hall and especially that of the Gare du Nord. For months on end I was, as far as colds are concerned, a runner-up to old Lagrume. By all means don't think that I'm complaining, that with vengeful pleasure I'm describing only the negative side. For I was very happy when I was on the beat. I enjoyed watching the so-called kleptomaniacs in the department stores. I felt that, one at a time, I was taking the next step in learning a profession of which I began to see the complexity more clearly every day.

Every time I enter the Gare de l'Est for instance, I can't help getting a heavy feeling. It always evokes scenes of mobilization for war. On the other hand, the Gare de Lyon as well as the Gare Montparnasse make me think of people going away on vacation. The Gare du Nord, the coldest, draftiest, busiest of all, recalls people's harsh and bitter struggle for daily bread. Is it because it is the gateway to the industrial and mining regions? In the morning the first night trains, arriving from Belgium and Germany, bring in the first load of crooks, of smugglers with faces hard as the light that falls through the dirty windowpanes. It is not just small fry. There are also the professionals of international grand larceny and smuggling, with their agents, their strawmen, their strong-arm men, all people who play for high stakes and are ready to defend themselves with every means at their disposal.

Hardly has this crowd flowed away, when it is the turn of the suburban trains, not the ones coming from the pleasant communities in the west or south of Paris, but from the unhealthy, grimy agglomerations of the north.

Les mémoires de Maigret

86

In the opposite direction, all those who for a great variety of reasons have to get out of the way try to make their escape to the nearest — the Belgian — frontier. In the grimy air of the platforms, smelling of smoke and sweat, hundreds of human beings are always waiting, getting excited, running from ticket window to luggage counter, studying lists of arrivals and departures, eating and drinking, surrounded by children, dogs, and canvas bags and suitcases. Nearly always they are people who have not had enough sleep, are nervous, afraid to miss their trains, often simply deadly afraid of what they will have to face elsewhere, the next day. Every day I spent hours and hours watching them, looking among all those faces for one face, more tense, eyes more fixed than the others. That of a man or a woman who is playing the last card. There stands their train. It will leave in just a few minutes. There are just those last hundred yards to cross, there is just that ticket that one clasps in one's hand to be checked. The hands of the enormous yellow clock move on jerkily. Heads or tails! Liberty or prison. Or worse . . . And there am I with a picture in my wallet or a description or perhaps nothing but the anatomical description of an ear. It happens that we spot one another at the very same second, that there is a real shock of

recognition, that we have understood one another
at exactly the same moment. What follows
depends on his character, on the risk he is running,
on his nervous system or some tiny material detail,
whether a door is open or locked or a suitcase
happens to stand between us. Some of them try to
flee and then follows the desperate pursuit
through groups of people who protest vociferously
or quickly get out of the way, through railroad
carriages, over railroad tracks and switches.
I have had two of them not three months apart,
and one of them still a boy, who reacted in
precisely the same way. One exactly like the other,
stuck their hands into their pockets as if looking
for a cigarette and a split-second later, right in the
middle of the crowd, with their eyes staring into
mine, they shot themselves through the head. They
didn't blame me any more than I blamed them.
Each one was doing his job. They had lost the
game, so they quit. But I too had lost the game,
because my job is to bring them to justice, alive.
I have seen thousands of trains depart. I have seen
thousands more arrive, each time in the same
atmosphere of excitement, with the same long
bustling lines of people running toward heavens
knows what.

Les mémoires de Maigret

89

At times he had asked himself if he couldn't give
fate a little push, hurry it up, maybe he hadn't
meant it seriously, but still . . . In his imagination
the catastrophe was bound to happen between the
Rue Choron at Montmartre and the church of
Notre-Dame-de-Lorette or maybe the church of
Trinité. He had his private geography, which only
made sense for him. The center of this geography
was the Rue Choron, a short, quiet street where
the only shop was one that sold newspapers and
cheap thrillers.

He couldn't go to the house in the Rue Choron
immediately after six o'clock, after locking up the
office, because it was already March and the days
were getting longer. The sun was still standing
between the chimneys of the houses. The streets
were still as crowded as at noon. Every year it
depressed him to see the days get longer, but
slowly as summer followed spring, he again got
used to his new timetable. Yet, his Friday evenings
only had their true flavor in the winter when the
streets were somber and cold, when he walked
through drizzle, fog or sleet, that surrounded the
street lights with an aura of mystery.

He only had another hundred yards to go and,
according to his ritual, he wanted to cross to the
other sidewalk. As he reached the middle of the
street, the only living being, he had a sudden
intuition of danger and just had time to turn his
head and see the two huge headlamps that
pounced on him, like enormous eyes which he
couldn't even try to escape, nor run away from.
Only his pupils dilated. Then he felt the impact
through his whole body. His head seemed to
explode. He was not aware of having yelled or
moaned. He was not aware of anything at all,
except of lying on the ground and seeing the stars
high above his head.

It had happened.

Was he dead? Was he going to die?

Une vie comme neuve

91

Two or three times he came to the door and I
must admit that I was beginning to get very scared
and I asked myself what would happen if once he
found me alone and noticed some money on the
table.
Now I am sure that he would not have had a
minute's hesitation and that they would have
found him after the crime in some ill-famed street,
sobering up and entertaining a few tarts with
long and pointless stories.

Les trois crimes de mes amis

Les mémoires de Maigret

What strikes me most, now that I am talking about these experiences, is the special relationship that springs up between the policeman and the criminal it is his job to track. First of all the cop, except in some special cases, is completely without hatred or even rancor. He is without pity in the sense that one usually attaches to that word. Our relationship, one could say, is a strictly professional one. We are on opposite sides of the barrier, that is perfectly clear and yet, up to a point, we are in the same boat. The prostitute on the Boulevard Clichy and the detective who is tailing her, both have leaky shoes and aching feet from having hiked over miles and miles of asphalt. They have been buffeted by the same downpour, the same icy wind. The night has the same color for both and they see with nearly identical eyes the shady character of the crowds milling around them.

It is not so different a situation from that of a pickpocket at the carnival. To him a fair, any mass of people, does not mean fun, carousel horses, circus tents, and doughnuts, but a certain number of wallets in accessible pockets. He and the policeman spot at a glance the self-satisfied provincial who makes the ideal victim.

Fifteen, twenty people were standing in front of the Black Marias. They were being pushed inside one by one. Some prostitutes, who were used to it, joked with the police, made obscene gestures at them and enjoyed themselves hugely. Others were sobbing. The men stood there with closed fists. One of them was a very blond youth with a shaven head. He had no papers at all and they had found a gun on him.

In the lodging houses and on the street the cops didn't do more than superficially frisk their catch. The real work was going to start at the police station, during the course of the night or even next morning.

"Papers, please."

The hotel-keepers were the most nervous of all, for they ran the risk of losing their permits. Of course there were irregularities everywhere. Each one of them had unregistered boarders.

"You know, inspector, that I have always been on the level. But what can you do? You get a customer after midnight and you're sleepy as hell . . ."

Maigret et son mort

95

For patrolman Jussiaume those comings and goings were an integral part of his routine. He registered them automatically, the way people who live near the railroad register the coming and going of trains. Wet sleet was falling and Jussiaume took shelter for a moment in a doorway on the corner of the Rue Fontaine and th : Rue Pigalle. The neon sign at Picratt's was one of the few in the neighborhood that was still on, throwing reflections like puddles of blood on the wet pavement. It was Monday, always a dead night at Montmartre. Jussiaume could have recalled the exact sequence in which the night clubs had closed their doors. He saw Picratt's sign go out in its turn. The owner, short and thick-set, with a beige raincoat thrown over his dinner jacket, came outside and started to turn down the steel shutter. A figure, it looked like a kid, slunk along the walls down the Rue Pigalle in the direction of the Rue Blanche. Then, two men, one of them with a saxophone case under his arm, climbed uphill, towards the Place Clichy.

Patrolman Jussiaume didn't know any of their names, he hardly knew their faces and yet those silhouettes and hundreds of others had some meaning to him. He knew that a woman was going to come out in her turn, wearing a light-colored, very short fur coat and that, perched on much too high stilletto heels she would almost break into a run, as if scared stiff of being all alone outside at four o'clock in the morning. She had only a hundred yards to go to reach the house where she lived. She had to ring the bell, because at that late hour the door was always locked.

Then the last two, they were always together, sauntered in muffled conversation up to the corner of the street and there they separated, just a few steps away from him. One, the oldest and tallest, swinging her hips, then walked up the Rue Pigalle as far as the Rue Lepic, where he had often seen her enter a house. She seemed to live there. The other one hesitated. She looked at him for a moment as if she wanted to tell him something. Then, instead of going down the Rue Notre-Dame-de-Lorette, as she usually did, she walked to the bar on the corner of the Rue de Douai, where the light was still on. She looked as if she had been drinking. She was hatless and her gold-blond hair glistened each time she passed under a streetlight. She walked slowly and stopped once or twice, as if she were talking to herself. The owner of the bar asked her familiarly:

"Coffee, Arlette? "

"With cognac! "

Maigret au 'Picratt's'

The streets were deserted and wet. A fine drizzle enclosed the streetlamps in halos. A few figures were moving close to the houses. On the corner of the Rue Montmartre and the great Boulevards, a café was still open. A bit further down they noticed the neon signs of two or three night clubs, where taxis were waiting along the sidewalk. A few steps away from the Place Blanche, the Place Vintimille was a little island of peace. A police car was standing at the curb. Near the grillwork of the tiny square, stood four or five men around a light-colored shape stretched out on the ground.

Maigret et la jeune morte

Basically he could not conceive of sex without tenderness and even a certain respect for one's partner, and he had remained cold with the professionals with whom he had sometimes tried to go to bed. What had attracted him towards them was not so much desire as the troubled atmosphere that surrounded them. The atmosphere you find, for instance, near the Boulevard Sébastopol in those narrow streets around Les Halles. There was a small, yellowish bulb, spreading its weak light at the door of a drab hotel where women, dressed in red or green shifts, or in even louder colors, whispered hoarsely to the passersby. He continued on his way, but he was intrigued and could imagine the narrow passageway, the squeaking stairs, the room with its iron bedstead, its sink or its washstand.

Le déménagement

Had she known the shady hotels of this district, where the girls stood guard, perched on their too-high stilletto heels, or the Boulevard Sébastopol, which she mentioned a number of times when she talked about her housemaids?

"When I lived in Nice . . ." she would say, or,

"That reminds me of Narbonne . . ."

She knew nearly all the cities of the South and she had a very special way of talking about them. She had not visited them as a tourist. She had no relatives there. She had never brought back a single knicknack, a single souvenir.

She must have been twenty, thirty, forty when the brothels were still in full swing and nobody even thought of closing them. That's where I could place her, I was almost certain. First as one of the girls, then as the Madame's right hand, still attractive and stylish.

She doesn't talk about women as other women do. She knows them in a more intimate, more physical way. She gives the impression of having seen them in the raw, in the naked light hurrying through crudely lit hallways to the lavatory from the room where their customer was already stepping into his trousers. The same look was in her eyes when I saw her look at her successive maids, and one day when she didn't know I was on the stairs, I heard her say to a little brunette, who left after two months:

"You, you had a man last night. I can smell it! "

So everyone is part of a hierarchy, has a way to the top open to him. She had climbed her way up with all the energy she could muster from the Porte Saint Martin via the brothels of Nice, of Béziers, and of Avignon, to the throne in her maturity, dressed in silk and loaded with jewels, as the Madame of one of the establishments around the Madeleine or the Rue de Richelieu . . .

L'homme au petit chien

A few minutes later Maigret and the
fat chief inspector from the Rue
des Saussaies passed from one
world to another as they went
through the modest door that
separates the Palace of Justice from
the Criminal Division.

Maigret et le voleur paresseux

"Tell me, judge, have you ever tried to put a dried pea up your nose? "

"I beg your pardon? "

"I said a dried pea. I remember we played with them as children. You should really try it and look in the mirror. The result is surprising. I bet that with a pea in one of your nostrils, you'd walk by people who see you every day and they would fail to recognize you. Nothing changes a facial expression more. The people who know one most intimately are the ones who are most confused by the smallest change. Now, you are well aware that the face of our man has been much more severely deformed than by putting a dried pea up his nose! Then there is something else you should not forget. People always have the greatest difficulty imagining that their neighbor on the same floor or their colleague in the office or the waiter who has been serving them lunch for years could possibly, suddenly change into something different from what he has always been, change for instance into an assassin or into a victim.

One constantly reads about crimes in the newspapers, but one imagines always that they can happen only in some other world, some other sphere, anywhere but in one's own street, never in one's own house."

"Have you any hope of being close to a solution? " the district attorney asked.

"I do indeed have hope of a solution sooner or later, sir. Let me see, have I told you everything? I still should mention the spot of varnish."

"What spot of varnish? "

"On the seat of the trousers. Let me add that Inspector Moeurs of the lab discovered that, although it is practically invisible. He asserts it is fresh varnish. He adds specifically that the varnish had been applied to a piece of furniture no longer than three or four days ago. I am already having the railway stations checked, starting with the Gare de Lyon."

"Why the Gare de Lyon? "

"Because it is more or less like an extension of the Bastille neighborhood."

"And why specifically a station? "

Maigret sighed. Good God, how to explain it to him! How can a district attorney be without even an elementary sense of reality. How on earth can those people, who have never set foot in a bar, in a betting shop, or on a race track, people who don't even know what it means to be "in the soup", pretend that they could possibly be competent in fathoming the criminal soul?

Maigret et son mort

106

The door of the little room opened. A puff of
scent reached him, a scent long out of fashion but
one that he remembered dearly, for his mother
had used it on Sundays before leaving for High
Mass. Old Jaquette had indeed dressed as if for a
High Mass. She wore a black silk dress with a high
black lace collar around her thin neck, a black hat
with white taffeta bows, and immaculate white
gloves. All that was missing was the missal in her
hands.

"It's my duty," he murmured, "to take you to
Headquarters."

He was ready to show her the arrest warrant, but
against his expectation, she showed neither
surprise nor indignation. Without a word she
crossed the kitchen, made sure that the gas was
turned off, went into the study to close the
windows, and locked the door. She went out first.
Wouldn't it have been ridiculous, contemptible, to
put handcuffs on that nearly seventy-five-year-old
woman?

Maigret opened the door of the car for her, then
sat down at her side.

"Don't use the siren."

Maigret et les vieillards

109

The house telephone rang. "Is that you, Maigret? Would you come to my office for a moment?" That was nothing extraordinary. Every day or at any rate nearly every day, apart from the daily report, the Big Chief called me one or more times to his office. I had known him since my childhood. He used to spend his vacations close to us in the Allier Department and had become a friend of my father's. And this Big Chief in my eyes was truly the Chief in every sense of the word. He was the one under whom I had set my first steps in the Criminal Division, the one who, without exactly giving me privileges, had followed me discreetly and from on high. He was the man whom I had seen in his black coat and bowler hat walk calmly and all alone under a hail of bullets to the door of the bungalow where Bonnot and his gang had, during two days, repelled the siege of the police and the *gendarmerie*.

Les mémoires de Maigret

Suddenly he missed the fragrances of the café on the Place Dauphine, the anise flavor of the apéritifs that belonged to the atmosphere of that day. He had hoped in vain to meet someone who would drag him along and so he had a guilty conscience when, alone, he climbed up the three steps of the café in front of which a long, low red sports car was parked; he looked at it with interest. Too bad! Dr. Pardon had told him to take care of his liver, but he had not forbidden him to take a little drink, just one drink after a few weeks of nearly total abstinence.

Near the bar he found familiar faces, at least a dozen men from the Criminal Division who had as little to do as he had himself and who had left early. From time to time that happened, a lull that lasted a few days. Nothing to do but what we call matters of routine. And then suddenly, hell breaks loose again and all kinds of drama explodes in ever-accelerating fury, giving nobody time to eat or breathe.

La colère de Maigret

He was made welcome. Room was made for him at the bar and pointing at the glasses of opaline colored drink, he grunted:

"Same for me . . ."

Brasserie Bd. du Palais

They had now reached the freight yard of Les Halles. They kept on walking; Nouchi didn't even ask where they were going.

The atmosphere was somehow spooky. Between the blackened, metallic harshness of the hangars, enormous lamps were swaying high above the street, spreading star-shaped, blinding white rays that hurt one's eyes, but hardly gave any light. The old narrow houses, painted in outlandish colors and overloaded with lettering, were crooked as on the limp backdrop of a stage. The scene was cut in half by a train on the side of the Rue Montmartre. Human figures were moving as if in slow motion from dark shadows into that cold glare that had to make do as light.

Stan had stopped. Nouchi was still holding on to his arm. They were watching an enormous yellow truck with a name painted on its side with an address and a telephone number in Nantes. The driver was busy adjusting something in his engine by the light of an emergency lamp. From time to time the engine roared and a shudder shook the entire enormous yellow carcass. Meanwhile, work was going on. Cabbages were thrown down by a man somewhere high up under a tarpaulin. Below, a second man was catching them. He was some kind of vagrant; he had wrapped himself in nondescript rags over layers of newspapers to keep warm. Each time the old man caught a cabbage, he trembled as if on the point of collapse. He froze for an instant, then threw his cabbage to a spindly youngster who looked like a student, who in turn threw it to the expert whose job it was to build neat piles of cabbages on the sidewalk. Each one worked for himself. The cabbages were pallid green and covered with tiny diamonds of ice that scratched one's hands.

Nobody had even noticed Stan, who had been standing there for a quarter of an hour. One could not have guessed what he was thinking or what he was waiting for. Finally he pushed Nouchi's hand off his arm. He took one, two steps. Then a third one and there he was, standing between the bum and the student. He caught the next cabbage, almost shyly, and threw it in his turn. He had become part of the chain. The vagrant glanced at him in distrust and grunted something. Didn't it mean that with one guy more there would be less pay for each? The student frowned, but for another reason. He had noticed Stan's tic and heard him count aloud in some foreign language, Russian or Polish.

"Thousand three hundred . . . three hundred and one, two . . . two thousand three hundred three . . ."

For Stan had been calculating averages. The load was about half done. "Two thousand four hundred twenty-two . . ."

The cabbages were big and heavy. All one could still see was cabbage and hear the noise of the trains shuttling, dropping off freight cars at various points. Across the street they were piling oranges into a narrow store until its walls threatened to burst. The smell of oranges filled the whole section of Les Halles.

"Two thousand five hundred thirty-one . . ."

Had he made a mistake? Had he skipped a thousand? Was that man over there with the notebook, the guy in black leggings and a velvet collar, the boss? Had he noticed Stan? If so, and if he let him go on, that meant he would get paid like the others.

'L'outlaw'

113

"Just wait for me here."

She went into a bar, where the usual measure was pushed in front of her. She swallowed it in one gulp, took the money out of the bag under her apron and threw it on the counter. It was a glorious morning, bursting with life. Everything was alive. Everything had color. Everything smelled good and it was as if one were drinking in the air instead of inhaling it.

"You're not tired, are you? "

"Oh no, Mum."

"What are you going to do before school? " For at half past six she already had parked her pushcart at the usual place opposite the fish shop, and she was not even the first one.

"Don't worry, I'll find something to do."

His head was turning. His legs felt weak; it had been too much. Slowly he climbed the dark stairs, pushed the door of the room where the twins were still asleep. In the kitchen his sister was lighting the stove for coffee.

"Has Vladimir left already? "

"Yes, five minutes ago. And you, where are you coming from? "

"I went along with Mum."

"To Les Halles? Did she let you? Are you hungry? "

"I've had fresh rolls."

"Lucky dog! "

Le Petit Saint

Bit by bit Louis discovered that the ties that bound Gabrielle to her children were much stronger than he would ever have thought. It wasn't the kind of mother-love people prate about and that they teach you in school. It was more as if, unknown to herself, the umbilical cord which had attached her to her children had never been completely severed.

"Funny, Louis, that you've started to paint pictures."

She rarely spoke about his painting to him. He was convinced that coming home, she looked at his paintings, but they had so little in common with what she imagined paintings should look like that she'd rather say nothing.

"Is it going to be your trade?"

"It's not a trade."

"Well, some people make a living at it. I knew an old guy in a wide-brimmed hat and a flowing polka-dot tie. He was a real specialist. I think it was before you were born. I wasn't too bad looking in those days. He tried to tell me I was beautiful and that I could make a living as an artists' model, doing nothing but lying down naked and keeping still. One day I went to his studio near Saint-Germain-des-Prés to pose. He didn't even touch me with his little finger. He hardly talked to me. I had to laugh all the time, I don't know why. I found it funny to be standing there with nothing on for hours at a stretch in front of a man who didn't even try anything. He gave me five francs and asked me to come back whenever I wanted to. He made a good living at it and he not only had a studio, but also a lovely apartment with a big balcony and fine furniture."

Didn't she feel tempted to add: "Why don't you paint like him?"

Le Petit Saint

The vegetable growers, the farmers, the jobbers,
and their helpers give nothing for nothing and so
they must carefully watch the chain of men
unloading and stacking vegetables and fruits in
crates and in bulk, butter, fowl and all else that is
edible in neat piles on sidewalks and pavements as
the night proceeds. Still you can always find a
loophole, and I have always been able to wangle
into a crew and in the end to get paid enough to
eat.

The second night, towards dawn, just before
closing time, I discovered Barderini making his
purchases. He had a thick red scarf around his
neck; I made sure he wouldn't notice me.
Something that is part of Les Halles is that the
people who work in them, those who do the
buying and selling, are mostly not so very different
in origin from those who do the heavy manual
labor. Besides, no one pays here by check. Wealth
is not expressed abstractly, by symbols, but by
pulling large bundles of banknotes out of one's
pocket.

They all meet in that comparatively small number
of cafés with frosted-glass windows, where a
smell of country and of unwashed feet always
hangs in the air. They drink coffee, grog, red wine,
applejack, brandy, the whole spectrum of drinks.
They lean against the bar or sit at the few tables.
Others hang around against the walls, vaguely
waiting, half asleep. Here repugnance is unknown.
Dirt, infirmities, and illness are words without
meaning. One takes all possible deformities, all
deviations, all congenital defects for granted,
without pity but also without aversion.

Le passage de la ligne

At last, at five to twelve came Janvier's call.
"I'm in a hurry, boss. I'm afraid our bird could get
away again. I can see him through the little
window of the phone booth. I'm here at the
Yellow Dwarf bar, Boulevard Rochechouart . . .
Yes . . . He's spotted me. He certainly has
something on his conscience. He threw something
into the Seine when he crossed the bridge . . . At
least ten times he has tried to shake me off . . .
Shall I wait for you? "

And so started a chase, which would go on for five
days and five nights, all across a Paris which
realized nothing, through crowds of passersby,
from bar to bar, from café to café. On the one
hand, a man all by himself, on the other, Inspector
Maigret and his detectives in relays, who, if all is
said, were as harassed as the man they were
tracking.

Maigret jumped from a taxi opposite the Yellow
Dwarf at the cocktail hour and found Janvier
leaning on the bar. He didn't even try to take on
an innocent expression. On the contrary!

L'homme dans la rue

Simenon has often mentioned a certain bottle, which according to him could always be found in our sideboard on the Boulevard Richard-Lenoir—and indeed one can still find it there. My sister-in-law—it has become a hallowed tradition on her yearly visit from Alsace—always brings us a new supply.

He writes negligently that it is plum brandy. Well, it isn't, it is raspberry brandy and that, for people from Alsace, makes a crucial difference.

"I have corrected him at last, Louise. Now your sister can be happy! "

Les mémoires de Maigret

123

ICI
MON LUBLINER
STAND 260

280 fr.

Bistrot aux Puces

It goes back as far as July, on a weekday, I don't remember which one. I drove with her to Saint-Cloud to have lunch in one of those little garden restaurants which she loves. It was crowded. I only paid scant attention to two young men without jackets, one with very curly brown hair, sitting at the table next to us and looking constantly in our direction. I had an important appointment at half past two and at two o'clock we hadn't even started with our dessert. I told Yvette that I had to leave.

She asked: "May I stay?"

She didn't mention it the next day nor the day after. But three days later, when the light was already switched off and we were on the point of falling asleep, she asked: "Are you asleep, Lucien?"

"No."

"Can I say something?"

"Of course you can say something. Shall I switch on the light?"

"No. I think I have done something naughty again."

I have often asked myself whether her sincerity, her mania for confession, was a matter of qualms or one of natural sadism. Or was it perhaps her need to make her life interesting and give it the coloring of drama?

"Didn't you notice those two young men the other day at Saint-Cloud?"

"What young men?"

"The ones at the table next to ours. One of them was very muscular and had brown hair."

"Oh, yes."

"As soon as you were gone I noticed that he wanted to talk to me, for I saw him trying to get rid of his friend and sure enough a bit later he came over and asked me if he could join me for coffee."

En cas de malheur

She noticed faces very close by or very
far away, hair, eyes, noses, mouths
that moved. She heard voices that
didn't always seem to come out of
those mouths. She tried to realize,
without really succeeding, what type
of joint she was in. And automatically
she would grab her Scotch: "Your
health!"
Behind the bar was a blonde barmaid
with large breasts. She had always
wanted desperately to have breasts like
that when she was little. There was
also a black man in a white cap who
kept coming out of one door after the
other always grinning and whom
everybody seemed to know. And then
there was that American captain, who
was leaning against the bar, keeping his
glass in his hand without ever putting
it down, staring at her all the time.

Betty

127

Le suspect

A rawboned girl, who smelled of the country, went from table to table. She had something very motherly about her, although she could not be more than twenty-four or twenty-five years old. "Bean stew for you?"

The owner wore a blue apron. Without the least aggressiveness, people pushed their neighbors a bit out of the way in order to get more elbow room. Everybody was hungry. The tart red wine made one's lips pucker and cooperated with the stove in making the cheeks glow. Forks clinked against the thick earthenware. Gravy stains soaked the paper tablecloths more and more. The street, on the other side of windows flanked by evergreens in tubs, lay empty, absolutely empty: the white wall opposite with the words "Post no bills" stood ablaze in the intense sunshine.

"We went from bar to bar, the meanest, lowest, most dismal ones, where Bob loved the atmosphere and where he was fond of listening to the people chatting at the counter, workmen in overalls, little shopkeepers from the neighborhood, who came in for a quickie. We took most of our meals in those little simple restaurants, where the bill of fare is written on a slate and where the smell of fried onions always hangs in the air. In the evening, in our living room he started to write. He told me he was just making notes, but later he admitted that he was really writing a novel. He just wanted to make something, make something all by himself, whatever it was. He would have loved to describe Paris with its common people as he saw it. One day in a bar on the Place Blanche he muttered: 'I wouldn't mind a bit being a barman in a place like this . . .' He was angry, for I started to laugh. But I really thought that he was just joking."

Le grand Bob

Would Premier Chalamont, according to the tradition, get his political friends together in one of Paris' most elegant restaurants where, during the dessert, the guidelines of his new cabinet's policy would be unveiled?

In the President's day these gatherings had nearly always taken place in the private rooms of the restaurant Foyot near the Senate or at Lapérouse. Former cabinet members met again and exchanged their memories of previous ministries. Political hacks once more were offered the less important cabinet posts. There were usually some greenhorns around who, not yet familiar with the ritual, kept observing the veterans closely.

Even the voice sounds, the clatter of forks, knives and glasses during those lunches had a particular tonal quality, and the headwaiters, who knew all the guests, participated by their carefully measured deference and their conspiratorial smiles in the redistribution of cabinet posts.

Le président

L'homme qui regardait passer les trains

A few tables away from him, a portly man, his dinner jacket a trifle tight, impressive with his watch chain and his lacquered mustache, was seated as if enthroned. From the conversation Kees decided that he must be a city councilor or something of that kind. His wife, no less impressive, was wrapped in a black silk dress, on which she displayed, as in a showcase, lots of genuine or imitation diamonds. On the man's left sat their daughter, who resembled both of them and yet was not too unappetizing.

131

"I hope," he said, "that you're not going to take me once more to the Dindon farci for one of your legendary eating orgies! " This meant that he really looked forward to it. They went right around the corner to one of the best restaurants of Paris, frequented especially at lunchtime by stockbrokers, politicians, and from time to time, some cabinet minister or an all-powerful newspaper publisher. "A table for M. François! " the headwaiter called. François never forgot to shake hands with him. Of course, even here there were a certain number of people who refused to acknowledge the presence of the publisher of the scandal sheet *La Cravache* (*The Horsewhip*), but there were at least as many if not more who called him *"Cher ami."*

In the long run François, for his part, had learned to pronounce those very words in the appropriate tone of voice and to use them with people who, a short while ago, he would nervously have addressed as *"Monsieur le Directeur."* He knew how to shake hands in an easy manner, mixed with just the proper amount of respect, with cabinet ministers and senators.

Elegant restaurants did not bore him yet. They probably never would. He just loved to watch the heavy silver cart on which roast beef or spring lamb was carved and he always enjoyed thoroughly having the finest *hors d'oeuvres* delicately placed on the plate in front of him.

Les quatre jours d'un pauvre homme

It was a funny trade! They were like actors on stage. For hours on end each day his wife and he could hardly exchange a glance or a few mumbled words. One had to smile, to listen to funny stories and to confidences. At the age of forty-nine he already began to have the same gait as old Joseph. Most headwaiters and waiters, most restaurant owners, end up with flat feet. The world around them is not the same world as other people see. It is a world of numbered tables, of faces one knows or doesn't know, of menus, of certain specialties, of bills. For the last twenty years he had seen on the same *hors d'oeuvres* cart, in the same order, the same concoctions with fancy names that gave them their gourmet appeal. His gesture of presenting the menu never varied, nor the pantomime of preciously pouring the first drops of Gamay d'Auvergne, of Chanturgues, of white Rosé de Corent or of Sauvagnat into the host's glass. The customer then took a little sip of the liquid pretending to be a connoisseur who really knew his wines, clicked his tongue, and gave him a conspiratorial wink.

La mort d'Auguste

134

"Drink, for God's sake! "

He was accustomed to stop drinking precisely in time. But in the
theatre he had swallowed, without realizing it, much more than his
usual dose of cognac. He began to feel unsteady and he was aware
that everybody was looking at him, that people were watching him
with contempt—or with pity, which was even worse—watching
the great actor Maugin getting stewed.

"Let me tell you something, young man . . ."

"Yes, sir."

"You're just a dirty little bastard and you make me sick! Here
waiter, take what I owe you."

Once outside he heard steps behind him, and perhaps he would have
started to run if a cruising taxi had not stopped at the right moment.
It happened as it does in a dream or in a film scene that is carefully
directed. He was just in time pulling the cab door shut in the
stupified face of Cadot.

"Where do you want to go, M. Maugin? "

The driver knew him, of course, everybody knew his face.

"Please yourself. Who cares? Somewhere, nowhere."

And at that moment those words sounded sublime to him.

"Who cares? Somewhere, nowhere." He repeated the words softly
for himself, ruminated them, alone in his clammy corner, as if they
explained at last the woeful mystery of the universe.

Les volets verts

Les anneaux de Bicêtre

Professor Besson d'Argoulet, without knowing it, had started the tradition. Maugras had just become a Knight of the Legion of Honor and Besson, who already wore the decoration, was allowed to confer the medal on him. He couldn't resist the temptation. He loved all ceremonies, honors, titles, medals. And what he no doubt enjoyed most of all in his role as Head of the Department was to parade through the wards of the Brousset Hospital, followed by a retinue of a few dozen respectful students. It was a long time ago that they had left the Place Blanche and the Brasserie Graf behind them. There was actually no homogeneous group, for each one of them had gone his own way and they just met by chance, as people do in the bustle of Paris life. "Look who is here! And what has become of you? "

Many of these successful men would lunch at the Grand Véfour restaurant under the arcades of the Palais Royal. After he had become editor in chief Maugras often lunched in the room downstairs, where he had a reserved table. One day Besson gave him a call at his office. "Are you free for lunch next Tuesday? "

He had said yes without thinking anything of it, and when he arrived that Tuesday at the restaurant, he was surprised to hear the owner say: "The gentlemen are waiting for you upstairs." They had prepared a surprise party for him. Besson had got together some of their oldest friends, those who had made the grade, to celebrate his decoration. They had decided not to invite the ladies.

Les anneaux de Bicêtre

"How old do you think he was? " Those under forty would consider it quite normal for him to die at fifty-four. The older ones would at most feel a moment of anxiety, which would soon disappear. As far as Lina was concerned, she would be brokenhearted and so no doubt she would appeal to the bottle and, as had happened so often, the house physician of the Georges V would be called to give her a shot and let her sleep it off. She would get used to it. He was not at all indispensable to her. He even asked himself whether he had not rather harmed her and whether she would not be happier, more balanced, once a widow. Only one of the three women who had played a role in his life had escaped unscathed. Hélène Portal, a journalist, who still worked for him and who had steadfastly refused to marry him. Anxious to preserve her own personality, she had never wanted to really live with him, and for years they had kept separate apartments, separate circles of friends.

He really felt the need to lie there thinking, quietly, without being disturbed, without people trying to interrupt his interior monologue. It was not so much a matter of conscience, nor did he try to make up his balance sheet. He felt more as if he were leafing through a picture book of his life, without even trying to do it in chronological order.

138

La tête d'un homme

Mrs. Henderson, widow of an American diplomat with connections to the great banking families, lived alone in her villa. Since her husband's death, the ground floor was no longer used. She had only one servant, Elise Chatrier, who was more a lady's companion than a housekeeper. Twice a week the gardener came from Saint-Cloud to take care of the grounds around the villa. Hardly ever were there any visitors.

141

La colère de Maigret

"Let me talk with my apartment . . . hello . . . you there? " As if he didn't recognize her voice, as if it could be anyone but her! "Do you remember what time the trains leave for Morsang? . . . Yes, today, if possible before dinner . . . five fifty-two? . . . Wouldn't you like to go there tonight and stay tomorrow? . . . Good! Pack the little suitcase . . . no . . . I'll call them up myself . . ."

It was a country hotel, *Le Vieux Garçon*, on the banks of the Seine, a few miles above Corbeille. For the last twenty years the Maigrets had from time to time gone there for the weekend. Maigret had discovered it during one of his inquiries. It was isolated on the riverside and the guests were mostly people who came there for the fishing.

144

It was one of those Sundays that one
only remembers from childhood, all
radiance, everything looked like new,
from the sky blue as a jay to the
elongated reflections of the houses in
the water. Even the taxis looked a
more intense red and green than usual
and the empty streets were like
sound-boxes, which gaily echoed the
faintest noise.

L'écluse n⁰. 1

L'homme au petit chien

It has been raining heavily since yesterday afternoon, it's coming down in those heavy cold drops that blacken the house fronts, stream down the windowpanes and make the gutters overflow; wherever one turns, the sky is completely overcast. It is so dark that this morning the lights are on behind all windows. I don't mind at all when it rains on Sundays. Not because I am envious of the people who, at the first ray of sun, rush to the countryside. I have owned a car, even several at a time. I know the roads to Deauville and Le Touquet, the highways to the South and all good restaurants along the way. No, I am not jealous of anybody. If I don't mind streaming rain on the day that people are off, it is because I like the feeling that all those boxes are full, that all those houses are filled to the brim with human life.

147

"Are you going to the office?" my wife asked while I finished my cup of coffee standing up. I said yes. I just hate Sundays, especially Parisian sundays. They give me the creeps, they make me panicky. The very thought of having to stand in line holding an umbrella in front of some movie theatre makes me sick. Just as it nauseates me to stroll along the Champs-Elysées or through the Tuileries or to be caught in an endless line of cars on the road to Fontainebleau.

En cas de malheur

The sun was setting at last in fiery splendor, touching the faces of the passersby with a deep red glow which for a moment gave them a strange air of exaltation. The shadows of the trees had become denser. One could hear the murmurings of the Seine. Sounds carried farther and people already in bed noticed, as they do during the night, the ground vibrating under the passing buses.

Four times Madame Jeanne went upstairs to where Monsieur Bouvet lay very quietly in his apartment behind the drawn shades. Each time she felt the same satisfaction, for she was convinced that that was exactly what he would have liked her to do. Tomorrow morning, before the funeral, she would once more dust the room and give a quick polish to the red stone tiles. She opened the window a bit, for just a minute or two.

L'enterrement de M. Bouvet

To his mother, as to many other people of the neighborhood, himself included nowadays, the rest of Paris was foreign territory. He remembered the answer of his mother to someone who came into her little caretaker's office to ask for some information. He had been playing on the floor. "Oh, but that is on the other side of the square, in the fourth arrondissement." The Place des Vosges was located half in the fourth, the other half in the third arrondissement and she had said it as if she were speaking of a national boundary. He himself was nearly an emigrant, for while born in the fourth on the side of the Rue Saint-Antoine, he had lived in the third arrondissement ever since he got married.

While he was eating, Bob was visibly thinking.
"Is Uncle Marcel rich? "
"Very rich."
"And that new uncle who came here yesterday? "
"I don't think he is."
"Is he poor? "
"No, I don't think he is poor either."
"Like us? "
"We are only poor for the moment, Bob. By accident. Until I find a new job."
"I know."
"You've always had all you needed, haven't you? "
"Yes."
"Who told you we are poor? "
"Nobody."
"The shopkeepers? "
"No, Dad."
"Did the caretaker say anything to you? "
"No, she never talks to me."
"So who did? "
"Oh, it's so long ago."
"Who? "
"Mum."
"Did you have fun this morning? "
"No, we could hardly play. The girls were in the yard."
"Why didn't you play with the girls then? "
"I don't like girls. Boys never like girls."
Since the vacation had started a few days earlier, keeping the kid busy had been a real problem.
"I want you to stay home this afternoon, Bob. There must be plenty of books you have not read."
"Why do you want me to stay home? "
"I have to go to the hospital."
"But this is not a visiting day."
"Your mother had an operation this morning."
"Again? And why can't I come along? "
He couldn't very well answer: "Because your mother is perhaps already dead."

La porte

Les quatre jours d'un pauvre homme

Les quatre jours d'un pauvre homme

"The crowning glory of a wife's career, the logical apotheosis, is to be a widow! " Raoul had mocked. "I for one have had two wives. I don't know why on earth I ever married them, but at any rate I took care to leave them in time. A widower, that's something quite different. It had something indecent about it and when I was small I was convinced that a widower was something that smelled bad. I must have heard mother say something like that. She didn't like men in general and, lucky for her, she had more than her share of widowhood. Altogether, if one takes the trouble to calculate it, she has lived just as long as a widow as she did as a married woman."

155

"Let's take the Boulevard de Courcelles . . ." He was checking the house numbers. Number 24 was just across from the main entrance of the Monceau Park with its ornamental grillwork fences and its gilded spearpoints. Shouts of playing children, watched over by an attendant in a blue uniform, filled the air. It was a very imposing house. The enormous, very high carriage entrance was guarded by two men. One could well imagine how, long ago, coaches drawn by prancing horses had rolled onto the courtyard, where the stables had now been rebuilt as garages.

Maigret se défend

It was like a Sunday in his childhood. His parents
had made their plan. They would go, for instance,
to have lunch along the Seine and for reasons of
thrift, of course, would take a picnic along. They
had to go on foot, for they had no car. They had
to clamber across sandpits.

"Watch the puddles, Emile . . ."

How he would have loved to go and eat fried fish
in one of the open-air restaurants like everybody
else! The grass they were sitting on was dusty and
had a disagreeable odor.

Why did it always have to end in a quarrel—either
before they left or in the middle of the
afternoon? His mother was nervous. She acted as
if she were afraid of her husband, yet in reality it
was he who gave in to all her wishes.

Le déménagement

159

"I feel like a glass of beer."
A glass of beer on a café terrace in Montmartre,
at the Cyrano, on the corner of that Rue Lepic,
which for quite a while Bob had found to be the
most human in the world. There I recognized the
small hotel where he had been living with Lulu.

Le grand Bob

"I don't quite know what to do, see what I mean?
The deputy has given me the order to return to the
scene of the crime and to wait for him there. I
didn't find the body. Two men of the park police
found him . . ."

"Where? "

"Excuse me? "

"I'm asking you where? "

"In the Bois de Boulogne . . . Route des
Poteaux . . . you know where it is? Not far from
the Porte Dauphine . . . It is not a very young man,
about my age. As far as I could judge, there was
nothing in the pockets, no papers at all . . . Of
course I have not shifted the body . . . I don't
know why, but there was something not quite
right, it seemed, so I thought I'd give you a
ring . . . that's none of the business of those guys
from the D.A.'s office . . ."

Maigret et le voleur paresseux

Maigret came down the stairs and found a taxi
with the engine running right in front of the door.
"Bois de Boulogne . . . you know the Route des
Poteaux?"

"It would be too bad if I didn't know where that
was after thirty-five years behind the wheel . . ."
That, in short, is how people console themselves
about getting old.

161

Every neighborhood of Paris, every social class has, so to speak, its own way of killing a man, as it has its own way of committing suicide. There are streets where people jump out of the window, others where they open the gas valves, and others still where they do it by swallowing barbiturates. And so in some neighborhoods they use the knife; there are others where blackjacks are popular, and those, like Montmartre, where guns dominate.

La colère de Maigret

The prisoner in cell number 11 would have liked to be able to reread the note once more which he had found three days before, stuck on the bottom of his food bowl, but he had chewed and swallowed it as the sender had ordered him to do. Even an hour ago he had still known it literally by heart, but now there were some details he couldn't for the life of him remember word for word. "On October 15 at 2:00 a.m. you will find the door of your cell open. The guard will be kept busy somewhere else. If you follow the route indicated on this sketch . . ." The man passed a clammy hand over his burning forehead, looked with terror at the pools of light and nearly cried out aloud when he heard steps. But those were on the other side of the wall, in the street. The prisoner groped along the wall, stopped because he had kicked away a pebble. He stood there listening intently and looked so pale, so absurd with those long, apelike arms swaying in empty space, that anywhere else one would have taken him for someone dead-drunk.

On the other side of the wall Maigret and the judge were waiting less than fifty yards from the still invisible prisoner.

La tête d'un homme

He was dead tired after a nearly sleepless night. A little later he would again be facing the hand-cuffed René Mauvis. Again, as had happened every day for the last two weeks, reporters and photographers would fill the lobby. He couldn't even send Mauvis back to his cell in the Santé prison in the evening for fear the mob would lynch him and so he kept him in a cell in the basement of the Palace of Justice. What did he know about Mauvis? Until his thirty-second year he had been a model bank clerk in a branch office on the great Boulevards and he had lived alone in a three-room apartment in the Rue de Turenne close to the Place des Vosges. Mauvis was a bachelor. The caretaker had never caught him coming home with a woman and his colleagues had never seen him with a girl friend. His only known passion was playing pool. This he did two or three evenings a week in a café on the Boulevard Beaumarchais.

Now he was accused of having strangled—within six months—two little boys in the woods at Saint-Germain, where, he asserted, he had never even set foot.

La mort d'Auguste

On the other side of the wall there was a similar cell in the Maximum Security section of the Santé prison. There, as in four other cells on Death Row, a man sentenced to die was waiting either for commutation or for the solemn little group that would come one night and lead him away without saying a word. And for the last five days the prisoner in that cell had been moaning all the time from minute to minute, a muffled continuous groaning, interrupted by loud sobbing and howls of revolt.

Not a sound came from the passages, the courtyards, from that whole enormous fortress called the Santé prison nor from the streets around it, nothing but the howls from cell number ten.

La tête d'un homme

It was not even dawn yet. In some buildings around the prison, lights were being switched on.
From somewhere came the clatter of a streetcar, then the sound of a car stopping, the slamming
of its door, steps of heavy boots, some whispered orders. A nervous journalist was scribbling on
his pad. A man looked away.
Radek jumped briskly out of the Black Maria, looked around with his pale blue eyes, which
shone in the gray dawn. He was being held on both sides, but he looked unruffled and started
to walk with long strides towards the scaffold.
Then suddenly he slipped on a patch of ice. He stumbled. The guards, taking it for a last
attempt at rebellion, quickly pulled him up. It had only taken a few seconds, yet perhaps this
fall was more agonizing than all the rest, unbearable especially because of the expression of
shame that appeared on the condemned man's face as he was pulled up. He had lost all his
dignity, all of that pride and haughtiness with which he had armed himself. His glance fell on
Maigret, whom he had begged to be present at his execution. The inspector tried to look away.
"So you have come . . ."
People were getting impatient. Their nerves were taut in a common wish to get it over with.
Then Radek turned around and looked at the patch of ice with a sardonic smile, pointed at the
guillotine and sneered: "Messed up again . . ."

La tête d'un homme

167

"It is not a question of excusing or approving or absolving criminals. It is not a question either of surrounding them with an aura of glamor as has been the fashion for quite a while. It is a question of looking at them matter-of-factly, as a reality and with understanding. Not with curiosity, because curiosity evaporates very quickly. And, of course, without loathing. After all, one has to look at criminals as human beings who do exist and whom for the health of society, for the protection of the established order we have somehow, as far as we can, to keep within certain limits and to punish if they trespass them. They know it very well themselves! In fact they don't even blame us. They often admit frankly: 'You're doing your job.' "

"What they exactly think of that job is something that I prefer not even to guess. Are you surprised that after twenty-five or thirty years of service one develops that rather heavy gait, that slightly dull, often empty way of looking at people? "

"Aren't you often sick of it? "

"No. And that is just the point. It is probably through my job that I have acquired a rather indestructible optimism. If I may paraphrase a favorite word of my catechism teacher I'd say: 'Superficial knowledge makes one recoil from people, profound knowledge makes one accept them.' It is precisely because I have seen unappetizing behavior of all varieties that I have been able to realize how often it is compensated for by so much plain courage, good will, and endurance.

"Absolute fiends are rare and those I have met, unfortunately, were operating outside of my reach, outside of our field of action."

Les mémoires de Maigret

It is a question of knowledge, of really knowing the milieu where a crime has been committed, knowing the mode of life, the habits, the morals, the reactions of all the people living in it, those who commit the crime, those who are its victims and those who are simply witnesses. One has to enter their world without being astonished by anything, as if one belonged and spoke their language naturally. This applies as well to a bar in La Villette or near the Porte d'Italie as it does to the underworld of the Arabs, of the Poles, the Italians, the sluts of Pigalle, or the bad boys from the Place des Ternes. It applies in the same way to the world of the race track, to that of the pool room, of the safe-crackers or the jewelry specialists. So you see that we are not wasting time by walking the streets year after year, climbing the stairs, or watching the shoplifters in the department stores. Like the shoemaker and the pastry cook, we need our years of apprenticeship with this difference that our apprenticeship takes just about a whole lifetime, because there is a practically infinite number of circles to get acquainted with.

Whores, pickpockets, card-sharks, hold-up men, check artists, immediately recognize one another. One could say the same thing about policemen after a good number of years on the job. It has nothing to do with heavy shoes or umbrellas. I believe you notice it in a particular expression around the eyes, in a certain reaction—or perhaps I should say absence of reaction—when faced with a particular type of human being, with particular varieties of misery, abnormality or deviation.

Whatever the novelists may say: the policeman is above all a professional. He is an official.

Les mémoires de Maigret

170

When he stepped from the bus at the Porte Saint-Martin, his mood
was as gray as the low-hanging sky. Heavy rain clouds were touching
the roofs. It was cold and he felt cold inside. People around him
were going miserably to work, dragged out of their warm beds. They
walked, hands in their pockets, their collars up, with red noses and
the eyes of sleepwalkers. The color everywhere was hard and ugly.
At the Theatre de la Renaissance he passed a woman in a coat of the
same bottle-green as the one in which Alice had died.

Antoine et Julie

During a number of years he had undertaken a
long-range project, the creation of a new typeface,
which would be named after him, as happens every
twenty-five or fifty years. In the printing-houses,
in the composing rooms one would speak
routinely about a "Jeantet" as one speaks about an
Elzévir, a Garamond, a Baskerville, a Futura . . .
A number of letters, very large, beautifully drawn
in India ink, were covering the walls.
He didn't look at them, he didn't look either at
the silvery tops of the buses which, seen from his
window, looked like whales, nor at the arch of the
Porte Saint-Denis, which the sun was coloring a
deep ochre. He sat down again resignedly. His
armchair had its own history. He had found it in
the Flea Market after many months of browsing.
Every piece of furniture had its history including
the standing clock with its metallic green face, an
early nineteenth-century period piece with Roman
numerals. Just then it was pointing at seven.

Le veuf

"In the fifteen years that I have lived under the
bridges, this is the first time that somebody has
attacked a bum. We vagrants are inoffensive people.
You know that as well as anybody . . ."
She liked the word and repeated it:
"Inoffensive . . . we don't even fight . . .
everybody respects everybody else's freedom . . . if
we didn't mind our own business, why should we
want to sleep under the bridges? . . ."
He looked at her with increased attention, saw
that her eyes were a little bloodshot, that her
complexion was more vivid than yesterday.
"Have you had a couple of drinks? "
"Enough to get over my hangover."
"What do your friends here say? "
"They don't say anything . . . when you have seen
everything in life, what is the fun of chatting? "

Maigret et le clochard

174

He couldn't even remember whether a market
took place on those sidewalks every day or a few
times a week. It was not just a food market, for
there were also stands from which clothing was
swinging on hooks. It must be very close, maybe a
hundred yards from the hospital where he was
now lying. He had often glanced in passing at the
gray buildings around the big courtyard, with a
portico guarded like an armory by men in
uniform. He had always assumed that one put only
old people here or the incurably ill, who could be
seen from the street walking alone or in silent
groups. And the insane of course. For wasn't
Bicêtre at the same time a hospital and an insane
asylum? He didn't feel in the least humiliated or
frightened being there now himself. He still had a
strange taste in his mouth, but apart from that,
yesterday's anesthesia had left his mind clear and
free . . .

Les anneaux de Bicêtre

175

Ever since the early morning a gale had been
blowing, which threatened to tear the tiles from
the roofs and which made the windows rattle. It
was as if someone was knocking at them
constantly. The ferryboat Newhaven-Dieppe had,
according to the radio, made a difficult crossing
and had been forced to make three tries before it
could enter the breakwaters of Dieppe. It had
nearly given up.
Nevertheless the President had insisted upon going
out for his customary walk at eleven o'clock, all
wrapped up in his ancient astrakhan greatcoat,
which had known all the international conferences
from London to Warsaw, from the Kremlin to
Ottawa.
"I suppose you don't really want to go out?"
Madame Blanche, his nurse, had protested, when
she found the old man all dressed to go out. She
knew very well that if he really wanted to, she
would not be able to dissuade him, but
nevertheless she took up the battle she knew was
lost in advance.
"But Doctor Gaffé told you just last night . . ."
"Is it my life or his?"

Le président

"Before you question him, let me tell you how I
put my hands on him. I walked into a bar at the
Rue Blondel two steps away from the Porte Saint-
Martin. It also serves as a pool room. It is called
Chez Fernand. Fernand is an ex-jockey whom I
know well. So I show him a picture of M. Louis
and he looks at it as if he recognized him.
So I ask him, 'That one of your customers?'
'Not him, he isn't. But he has come here two or
three times with one of my regulars.'
'Who?'
'Fred the Clown.'
'The Acrobat? I thought he had been dead a long
time or in the clink!'
'Oh no, he is alive all right! He comes here every
afternoon for a drink and to play the horses. Come
to think of it, I haven't seen him for a couple of
days . . .'"

Maigret et l'homme du banc

"And so I found out that each time my brother
came to see me, he had also gone to see my late
husband at the office in the Rue Saint-Gothard or
somewhere else, I don't know where. He probably
waited for him in the street as he did for me . . ."
"Your husband never mentioned it to you, did
he? "
"No, he didn't want to make me unhappy and
that's why I never talked to him about it either. If
we had been more frank with one another, maybe
nothing ever would have happened. I have thought
a great deal about it . . . Wednesday, a bit before
noon, the telephone rang and I recognized my
brother's voice immediately . . . He told me he
absolutely had to see me, that it was a matter of
life or death and that this would be the last time
we would hear from him. Then we arranged to
meet, you know where. On my way to the hair-
dresser I went there. He was even more panicky
than the other times. He confessed that he had
done something very stupid without explaining
what he meant, but he implied that he might be
arrested any time. He needed a large sum of
money in order to be able to get away to Latin
America. I took all the money I had taken along
out of my purse and gave it to him . . ."

Maigret et les braves gens

179

On the right, in a puddle of moonlight, barges were floating. Water trickled through a badly closed floodgate of the lock and that produced the only sound under a sky that was calmer and deeper than a lake.

In two locals on either side of the street, the lights were still on. In the one, five men were playing cards, relaxed and without saying a word. Three of them wore sailors caps and the owner, at their table, was in his shirt-sleeves. In the other pub there was no card game going on. Three men were sitting around a table, looking sleepily into their glasses of brandy. There hung a dim light and it smelled of sleep. The mustached barkeeper in his blue sweater yawned from time to time, then he moved his arm to grasp his glass again. Opposite him sat a little man. The hair on his hands and face was as rough and yellow as bad hay. He looked sad or benumbed or perhaps drunk. His light transparent pupils were swimming in troubled fluid and he was shaking his head slowly and repeatedly as if he were nodding approval at his interior monologue. Time flowed on without a sound, without the ticking of a clock. Next to the local was a row of dilapidated cottages in sad little gardens. There was no light. Then at number eight, all by itself, stood a six-story house, old and grimy, too narrow for its height. On the second floor a bit of light was filtering through the shutters. On the third floor, where there were no shutters, a yellow paper blind formed a rectangle of light. Along the banks of the canal lay heaps of stone and sand. Cranes and empty carts were standing about. Was somebody playing the piano somewhere? From where was it coming? A bit past number eight, set back, a wooden hut could be seen on which the word "Dancing" had been painted. There was no one dancing at the time, in fact there was no one but the fat woman behind the bar reading her newspaper and getting up every now and then to put a coin into the Pianola. Somebody or something had to move at a given moment. It was the hairy bargeman in the pub on the right. He had some trouble getting up, looked hard at the empty glasses and, searching his pockets, seemed busy with mental calculations. He counted his money, threw it on the smooth wooden tabletop, touched the visor of his cap and staggered to the door. The two others looked at one another. The owner gave a wink. The old bargeman's hand hesitated in space before grasping the doorknob and he swayed lightly when turning around to close the door behind him.

L'écluse n°. 1

As so often happens, they had overloaded their
barge and the day before while leaving the harbor
of La Villette to enter the Canal Saint-Martin they
had scraped the mud at the bottom. The doors of
the lock opened. Jules was standing at the rudder.
His brother had gone ashore to slip the lanyards
off the hooks. The screw started to turn and, as
they had both feared, it stirred up a thick cloud of
mud which rose to the surface in big dirty bubbles.
Robert threw his full weight on the pole to keep
the bow of the barge away from the bank. It
looked as if the screw was turning free, without
even touching the water. The lock-keeper, used to
it all, stood waiting patiently, hitting his palms together trying to keep warm.

There was a shock, followed by an ominous grinding of gears and Robert Naud turned to his brother, who immediately switched off the engine. Neither of them knew what had happened. The screw had not touched bottom for it was protected by part of the rudder. Something must have got entangled in it. Maybe one of the old cables that always lie about on the bottom of canals. If that was it, they would have a hard job getting rid of it. Robert walked with his pole to the stern, bent over and tried to locate the screw under the opaque water. Meanwhile Jules went looking for a smaller boat hook, as his wife stuck her head out of the hatchway.

"What is it? "

"No idea."

They started silently to work with both boat hooks around the stalled screw and after a few minutes Dambois, the lock-keeper whom everybody called Charlie, came to watch how they were doing from the quay. He didn't ask any questions, but stood there, mute, puffing his pipe, which was held together with a piece of string.

"Got it? "

"Think so."

"A cable? "

"Who knows? "

Jules Naud had caught some object in his boat hook and after a while, when the thing let go, new bubbles of air came to the surface. Slowly he withdrew his pole and when the hook had reached the surface, one saw dangling from it a strange package from which the newspapers—held together with string—had partly decayed. It was a human arm, a whole arm from hand to shoulder. In the water it had taken on the pallid color and the texture of dead fish.

Maigret et le corps sans tête

183

It was one of those little cafés one can still find, not in Paris itself, but in the old suburbs, a little café from a picture postcard or perhaps from an Utrillo painting. The house had only one story and actually constituted the corner. It had a dirty red tile roof and was painted yellow; on it was in large brown letters Au Petit Albert, and on either side, surrounded by naive arabesques: "Wines–Kitchen open 24 hours." In the courtyard behind the café in a shed the inspector found the tubs with evergreens, which during the summer no doubt were placed outside with two or three metal tables to form the terrace. Maigret already felt at home in the empty house. There had been no heat for the last few days and so the air was cold and humid. He kept eyeing the big stove that stood in the middle of the café with its black gleaming stovepipe that ran across the space before disappearing into the wall. After all, why not? There was plenty of coal in the shute. In the same shed in the yard he found some firewood next to a hatchet and a block. In a corner of the kitchen lay old newspapers. A few minutes later the fire was roaring and the inspector was standing in front of the stove with his hands behind his back in his usual pose.

Maigret et son mort

185

In general the drawings depict actual locations referred to in the text. In some cases as for instance numbers 28, 32, 55, 64, 95, 112, 124, I drew a similar atmosphere but in a different spot from the one described. For the benefit of Paris devotees I list here all actual locations.

2, 3	*Place Furstenberg*
6, 7	*Ecluse de Suresnes*
8	*Epalinges, en Suisse*
18, 19	*Place de l'Opéra*
20, 21	*Un Grand Boulevard*
22, 23	*Boulevard Richard-Lenoir*
24, 25	*Boulevard des Italiens*
27	*Boulevard Rochechouart*
28	*Galerie des Glaces, Versailles*
29	*Deux Métros*
30, 31	*La Madeleine*
32	*Le Quick-Elysées*
33	*Near the Sorbonne*
34, 35	*Place Saint-Germain-des-Prés*
36, 37	*The Notre-Dame*
38	*Bridges on the Seine*
40, 41	*Jardin du Luxembourg*
42	*Parc Monceau*
43	*Jardin du Luxembourg*
45	*Place Saint-Georges*
46	*Place du Tertre*
47	*Place des Abbesses*
48	*Montmartre*
50, 51	*Le Moulin-Rouge*
53	*Le Moulin-Rouge*
54	*Picratt's*
55	*Rue de Douai*
56, 57	*Boulevard du Montparnasse*
58, 59	*La Coupole*
60, 61	*Place Denfert-Rochereau*
62, 63	*Bakery*
64	*Rue Taitbout*
65	*The glazier*
68	*Rue de La Roquette*
72, 73	*Place Saint-Georges*
74	*Passage Choiseul*
75	*Rue Saint-Antoine*
76, 77	*Rue Lepic*
78, 79	*Rue de Grenelle*
80	*Police precinct, Les Halles district*
81	*Rue de Crimée*
82, 83	*Rue Fléchier*
85	*Rue Saint-Médard*
87	*Gare Saint-Lazare*
88	*Gare du Nord*
89	*Waiting room in the station*
90	*Rue Laffitte*

LIST OF BOOKS CITED

He had enough money, that much was true. But he was suspicious and he had put it in four or five different banks and had kept as much as possible in gold, which he went himself to put into his various safe deposit boxes.

But he was much less well-off than was generally believed and than the newspapers asserted with such exasperating satisfaction. Most of those astronomical figures were part of the bluff of the movie companies. The tax collector got the bulk of it anyway.

What everybody also seemed to forget was that only in the last ten years had the movies given him that large income. Until his fiftieth year he had lived only from the stage. Until his fortieth he had had trouble paying his bills. Until his thirtieth he had not had enough to eat.

Do you get that, my dear Count de Jonzé, who-finds-it-so-amusing-to-hang-around-with-bohemians!

Les volets verts

191

Il va sans dire que je continue à me balader à travers le Paris de Simenon en le dessinant

Mais hélas! il n'y a plus d'espace dans ce livre.

Au revoir, Paris!
Au revoir, Simenon!
Au revoir, amis!

Frederick Franck

LE PARIS DE SIMENON

Vous trouverez sur ce plan la plupart des titres des ouvrages de Simenon qui ont été cités dans notre album. Nous avons imprimé ces noms de lieux en italique : ils figurent au centre des quartiers où se joue principalement l'action des romans évoqués.

AVENUE

B. VICTOR HUGO

AVENUE DE NEUILLY

AVENUE DES TERNES

BOULEVARD

WAGRAM

DE

PL. VILLIERS

B. D

B. DE COURCELLES

MALESHERBES

PARC DE MONCEAU

AV. DE LA GRANDE ARMEE

AVENUE

RUE

DU

Maigret se défend

Les volets verts

PLACE DE L'ETOILE

AV. DE FRIEDLAND

BOULEV

FAUBOURG

AV. R. POINCARE

AV. R.

AVENUE KLEBER

AVENUE

AV. GEORGE-V

DES

SAINT

CHAMPS-ELYSEES

RUE

RUE DE LA FAISANDERIE

DE

LONGCHAMP

R. BELLES FEUILLES

Le déménagement
Monsieur la Souris
L'homme qui regardait passer les trains

GR. PALAIS

PT. PALAIS

BOIS

RUE DE LA POMPE

PL. DU TROCADERO

PT. DE L'ALMA

QUAI D'ORSAY

PT. ALEXANDRE-III

PT. D.

DE BOULOGNE

RUE DE LA TOUR

R. FRANKLIN

PALAIS DE CHAILLOT

AVENUE DE NEW YORK

BRANLY

PL. DES INVALIDES

Le p

QUAI

PT. D'IENA

TOUR EIFFEL

B. DE BEAUSEJOUR

M M L

PT. BIR-HAKEIM

AVENUE DE SUFFREN

B. DES INVALIDES

QUAI DE PASSY

B. DE MONTMORENCY

QUAI DE GRENELLE

B. DE

CHAMP-DE-MARS

AV. DE LA MOTTE-PICQUET

GRENELLE

RUE D'AUTEUIL

R. REMUSAT

PONT MIRABEAU

AVENUE

RUE

R. DES ENTREPRENEURS

EMILE

ZOLA

R. FREMICOURT

B. DE GARIBALDI

RUE

DE

VERSAILLES

DE

RUE DE JAVEL

RUE DU COMMERCE

RUE MADEMOISELLE

La tête d'un homme

AVENUE

PONT D'AUTEUIL

RUE

RUE DE

VAUGIRARD

BOULEVARD VICTOR

RUE

RUE DE LA PROCESSION